Margaret and Me

A Spirited Tale of Terror

Foreword

This book is an account of my experiences and development of my life as a psychic and investigator of the paranormal. Now as you read through these short stories you may wonder if these events are factual or the deranged fabrication of a deluded mind; it is up to you.

I have, as best as my memory can recall, given you a factual recollection of the experiences that I and others have encountered.

This book is a testimony that spirits of the dead are real, and that entities are real, and that evil does exist.

The battle between good and bad is raging all around us, however 99% of the human race is very much unaware of it.

If you are one of the one percent that gets drawn into the battle, then you have to decide which side you want to take.

No one can make that decision for you.

The names of those involved have been changed to protect their identities, and any perceived similarities are a coincidence.

I would like to thank all those who have been involved in helping to make this book possible and to thank you, as the reader, for supporting me.

As a wise man once said, "Do not pity the dead, but pity the living".

Enjoy reading this book but remember to ensure that you take precautions to protect yourself if you feel vulnerable or scared.

Burning sage acts as a protection or you may want to say the Lord's Prayer at night; just do what feels right for you.

This book is dedicated to my sisters Lorna, Sarah, Tracy, and Nicola who are, and always have been my biggest fans, and to my husband, Peter who loves and supports me no matter what, even when he doesn't fully understand what I do and why.

IN THE BEGINNING...

As Ann and I slowly crept up the stairs the torch I was holding slowly started to shake as my hand started to tremble. I could feel my chest getting tighter and tighter as if there was an invisible hand grasping at my heart.

I strained through the darkness trying to assess where Margaret was. She had gone upstairs to investigate the rooms above however, now, there was no sign of her.

Behind me I could hear my assistant Ann's breathing, she was struggling with the stairs being 8 months pregnant and being overweight.

'Are you two ok?' asked Mrs Renault, the owner of the house we were investigating.

'Yes', I answered, 'just trying to manoeuvre these stairs'. Winding stairs were not my favourite since you never know what is coming from around the corner. Anyway, moving on, I could see the torch light shaking as my hand started to tremble. I could feel that there was an uneasy presence around the stairs. I could tell from the vibration that this was a spirit of a dead person; the spirit of a person that has refused to cross over; a spirit that had a sense of vengeance and malice around them.

As I started to approach the final few steps, I felt a force like a large open hand pushing and pinning me to the wall. I was trapped and could not move. I looked over to Ann who was 3 stairs below me holding tight to a lit candle.

The shocked look on her face told me she was terrified. At that moment I saw her ginger ponytail lift into the air and with a yanking movement she fell sideways down the stairs.

'Oh my God' I yelled 'are you ok?' I shouted. 'Yes' she replied as she was being assisted back to her feet by Mrs Renault.

With all my strength I pulled myself off the wall and continued up the stairs knowing that there were two spirits we were going to have to deal with tonight, and these two spirits were not going to give up without a fight.

At the top of the stairs Margaret appeared and said, 'By the way, I think you should know there are two spirits here'!

'No shit Sherlock, Margaret! Now you tell me', was my answer.

Ok, I think I may have jumped the gun a little bit. As you have already gathered, I deal with and contact the spirit world and investigate hauntings. But how did all of this come about?

How did Mrs Renault know to call on me to deal with her haunted house?

To answer this, I think it would be good to start from the very beginning; how Margaret came into my life and how I discovered that I could see the spirits of the dead and other entities.

My first memory of seeing spirit came when I was around 6 years old. Being the only boy and having 4 sisters, I spent a lot of my time playing with my little soldiers; the little green ones that all have a set pose. I had the great gift of a creative imagination, losing myself in the world of playing army commandos with my little green plastic solders. I would build a town where there would be a King and Queen, a

Prime Minister and lots of people who would live inside the made up town out of house bricks. They would go about their business with a little task force keeping guard from enemy attack.

Now the fun would begin, and I would start throwing stones at the town to blow up the residents and try to take over the town with my little army of baddies. Lots of fun for an over-active 6-year old's mind.

I remember this day as clearly as if it was only yesterday. As I recall I was setting up the town on a very bright and sunny day, the heat from the sun warming my back. I had not noticed it at first but slowly I became aware of a shadow forming over the area where I was playing.

A silhouette of a person's shadow had appeared over the concrete where I was sitting. It was the shape of a very tall man.

At first I thought it was my father coming back from working on the farm. I turned round to see who it was but the sun was shining brightly in my eyes. Blinking through the rays I could see a bearded man who looked to be in his 60s peering down at me.

He was wearing a uniform very similar to the ones my little green soldiers were wearing. A little afraid I asked who he was and whether he wanted to speak to my mum. 'No, I want to speak to you' was his answer. I now became very nervous.

I was one of those children that was born and brought up in the time of 'Charlie Says'. A little boy and his evil looking cat called Charlie traumatised a whole generation in the 70s. They warned children about strangers with puppies who offered sweets in an attempt to kidnap the local children. Please check it out on YouTube if you don't know or remember 'Charlie Says'.

'It's ok Joseph I'm here to help and guide you. My name is Albert. I am an entity, or spirit and I'm here to tell you that you will start seeing many things that you will not understand; some of them will be good and will want to help you, and some of them are bad and will want to hurt you'.

At this time I guess I probably did not fully understand what he meant. I had lost that nervous feeling and had started to develop a sense of trust toward this Albert.

'Now Joseph, you will be assigned a spirit that will act as a guide, this spirit will help you to determine which spirits are good and which spirits are bad'

'Your guide will also help you to identify entities. These are beings that are not human souls.'

As you can well imagine this was going over the top of my head. I did not have a clue what this man was going on about or what he meant by the term 'entities'.

Albert looked down at me and with a look of darkness in his eyes confirmed to me that 'not all spirits are good'. And with a blink of my eyes he was gone.

No, there were no big revelations, no rays of heavenly light shining down upon me, just a very tall and miserable looking man with a beard, telling me that I was going to have lots of spirits visiting me.

After he had vanished, I ran into the house to tell my mother what had happened, however as you can imagine I was told not to be so daft and that I had to rein in my over-active imagination.

Now I think I should point out that at this time I was living in a family where my mother was (and indeed still is) a Jehovah's Witness, with the belief that spirits are not the souls of dead people but evil demons that went around hurting and deceiving people all working as part of the devil doing harm brigade.

Albert's visit played on my mind for a couple of days in which I would spend several hours waiting in the garden for him to re-appear. It was not until around a week later that something so terrible happened that it would change the course of my life forever. Even now as I am recalling this story the tiny hairs on my arms are standing on end. Living on a farm with very few streetlights you can imagine that the area where I lived would already be dark and creepy; even the house in which I lived gave off a feeling of something dark.

Lying in my bed in a room that was in the oldest part of a house which was over one hundred and fifty years old, I can remember having an uneasy feeling.

On the far wall I could see light from the moon shining in through the thin curtains, recreating the shape of the window on my wall.

Every now and then a small shadow would appear, maybe that of a bird or the branches of the tree in the garden. I don't know what they were, but I could feel myself getting more and more afraid; lots of scary thoughts churning inside my head.

I thought about characters that I had seen on the television such as the werewolf man and the mummy. Daft as it may seem to us as adults, watching these films at the age of six can have a toll on the mind!

Closing my eyes really tightly, I wished the scary thoughts would stop and for peace and calm to come into my mind. I contemplated jumping out of bed and running to my parents' room, but the fear of the werewolf man eating me made me stay put. I felt trapped and alone.

It was then that I heard the breathing. I strained my ears to focus on what I was hearing. Yes, it was breathing! The sound a person makes when they have a chest cold, a deep rattling and rasping breathing sound. I was able to pin-point that the sound was coming from the side of my bed.

I could make out that the breathing was moving up and down the length of the side of my bed. I closed my eyes tightly gritting my teeth in fear. The breathing became louder and more obvious.

My bedroom door was closed, and I knew that I was the only one in the room. I felt the bottom corner of my bed go down slightly with the blankets slowly pulling as if someone heavy was sitting on the corner.

I bravely opened one eye only enough to sneak a peek. There was no-one there, yet I could still feel the weight on the bed. I tightly closed my eyes and pulled the blanket over my head and pulled my knees to my chest.

Deafened by the sound of my own breathing and the thunderous beat of my little heart pumping in my chest, I could sense that something was now peering down over me, breathing closely on the blankets that now covered my head.

Gripped by fear, I could not bring myself to scream. For what seemed hours I lay there too terrified to move. Shall I run to mum and dad's room, or should I wait? Before I could act I felt an icy hand grasp my ankle and sharply pull on my leg. That was all I needed for my fight or flight response to kick in! I clambered out of bed and ran into my mum and dad's room, screaming like a wild banshee.

'There's a man in my bed' I screamed 'there's a man in my bed'! 'What the bloody hell is he going on about?' my dad responded. 'You know what he's like', answered my mother 'obviously his over-active imagination again'.

'I'm not going back in there' I yelled, 'there's a man breathing in my room. I want to stay here with you', I demanded.

Surprisingly, my father agreed to go and sleep in my room to prove that there was nothing there, and with that I settled in their bed and dropped off to sleep.

The next morning, I woke up feeling a little more relieved that I had been safe in my parents' bed. After getting up and dressed I went to go down to the kitchen to get breakfast. Halfway down the stairs I could hear my parents talking.

'I don't bloody know what it is, but there was breathing coming from under the bed' my father was confirming to my mother. I sat on the stairs shocked and scared, what was I going to do now?

For reasons unknown I agreed to go to bed in my own room that night. I can't even remember questioning or challenging my parents as to what was in my room. All I knew was that it was something which was not nice.

That night I did not hear the breathing, which was a huge relief and I fell asleep quickly, probably from being exhausted from the night before. It was half way through the night that I awoke startled. I could feel a heavy weight upon me. With my eyes open I could see above me the formation of a transparent bolder slowly being placed upon me.

An overwhelming fear surrounded me as if I was being crushed. It was then I could hear a voice in the room saying 'crush the witch crush her'. I managed to take a breath and let out a scream, which alerted my parents to come into my room,

'The rocks were crushing me', I cried after managing to get out of bed. Yes, you guessed it, their reply was 'it's your over-active imagination'! Very scared, I got back into the bed which was now damp due to the excess perspiration brought about from fear.

As a child I suffered several accounts of the crushing, but very quickly learnt to prevent it over time with the power of thought. It was only later that these experiences became clearer. I watched a film set in the sixteenth century on the subject of witchcraft. One of the villagers had been accused of witchcraft. After being found guilty the villagers killed the woman by crushing her under large rocks.

Apparently, this was a common practice in dealing with witches. It was believed that the crushing would crush the spirit of the devil out of the victim. I did not really understand why this was happening to me, but it helped me to develop a mechanism to switch these visions off from my mind.

During the subsequent school holidays a couple of months after my initial visit from

Albert, I recall going to bed late as I had stayed up with my mum. We were waiting for my sisters and father to come home from seeing 'Jaws' at the cinema. Naturally, I had wanted to go too, but I was too young.

I remember opening the door of my room and feeling a cold sensation coming over me. I turned on the light and walked in to my room. After I had walked a couple of feet, the door slammed shut behind me. I span around to see a short fat lady standing behind me.

'Don't scream' she said putting her finger to her mouth. 'Albert sent me; I'm the spirit who has been sent to look after you'.

For some unknown reason I was not afraid and did not react. I was calm. 'That's good' she said, 'I'm Margaret'. I could not reply; the words were not there. 'I am from the spirit world. I died about 300 years ago, I think' she walked over towards me, as clear as day she appeared in front me.

Margaret was a very odd-looking woman, round in shape with wild curly grey hair. She was dressed in long dirty dress, with old and worn-out boots. She was what you can imagine a fisherman's wife to look like.

Now contrary to what some people may believe, guides are not always Egyptian priests, Princesses or Red Indian chiefs. Margaret told me that spirit guides are ordinary people who have lived before. Spirit guides are assigned to people they can relate to. 'What would you have in common with an Egyptian priest?' she once asked me.

She sat on my bed and told me to get into bed and to listen to what she was going to tell me. There was a kindness in her face which was different from what I saw in the face of Albert.

'There are spirits here on the Earth that have not crossed over,' she began. 'It is not always clear why they choose to stay. Some may have been killed in such a terrible way that the spirit does not realise that they are dead. '

She told me that there some people that are so bad when they are alive that this evilness then prevents them from crossing over when they die. They now roam the earth tormenting others and being tormented.

'There are spirits like me that connect to people who have the gift of sight who help and guide the gifted', she said.

'Now don't be frightened' she implored looking me straight in the eye. 'There are things that have not been born of this world; these are evil beings that seek out to hurt and destroy people. However, there are also some spirit beings that will sit on the fence and have a foot in each camp." For some unknown reason, my thoughts were directed to Albert. 'I cannot protect you from these beings, but I can teach you to defend yourself from them and to detect them'.

Even at the age I was, I fully understood what she was saying. It was clear to me that things were never going to be the same again. Margaret said that she would not be with me all the time as this was not how it works; she would come and appear when needed.

Not all spiritual experiences involve actual spirits. I have added a short story next to show how an over-active imagination, fuelled by fear and experience of actually seeing spirit can set off a chain of events that are somewhat foolish and rather embarrassing. I should also add that I have spent a lifetime wreaking my revenge on my sister who was the instigator of this next story.

ARE FRUIT PASTILLES THE CURE FOR EVERYTHING?

This is a short story about one of those times when fear and over imagination can cause rather a lot of embarrassment and exaggeration. I would have been about seven years of age at the time, and I will admit I was your typical annoying little brother who just wanted to hang out with one of his big sisters.

Now my 3rd oldest sister had made it her life's mission to torment me and scare the living daylights out of me. This is something I now have great pleasure in getting her back for, a bit of tit for tat. It was around the summer holidays and my sister was out and about in the village with a couple of her own friends.

I was with them, as mum had probably told her to keep an eye on me. As I recall, we were heading back to the farm taking us through the local primary school and church yard.

Blakedown First School was rather old and creepy with an old church and graveyard attached and was a scary place at the best of times.

I remember you had to go through the creepy graveyard to get to the playing fields and the path that led home. I am under no illusion that my sister and her friends were scheming on a way to scare me. As we were walking past the graves the girls, being a few years older and much faster, were walking in front of me, with me toddling slowly behind.

It was then that it happened; my sister turned round and with a horrified look on her face she raised her hand and with her finger pointed towards me she screamed 'Oh my God, it's the headless Nun'. In unison the three of them started running through the graveyard, screaming and turning briefly shouting at me to "run.... run! She's right behind you!".

Terrified beyond compare and not being the most agile child, I ran as fast as my little bony legs would go, which wasn't fast. I could feel an icy cold chill at the back of my neck as I felt the spirit of the headless nun getting closer and closer. Screaming hysterically, I cried for my sister and her friends to wait for me and not to leave me to be killed by the ghost of the headless nun.

I think that it was around the third time they turned calling me to run faster that I lost control of my bladder and peed myself. As embarrassing as it is I am not ashamed to say how traumatised and scared I was at this point. I was sobbing uncontrollably and with snot pouring down my face, I finally caught up with them. Barely able to speak, as I was still sobbing and trying to breath as well as being soaking wet, I was relieved that the headless nun had not killed me.

After finding this all very hilarious my sister had finally come to the realisation that she was going to have to take me home and explain to our mother why I was soaking wet with urine, covered in green mucus, sobbing and unable to speak clear English.

Taking a half-eaten packet of Fruit Pastilles out of her pocket, she handed them to me asking me to promise not to tell mum what had happened. Still unable to speak I nodded in agreement.

It's funny really, but half a packet of fruit pastilles was unable to have the miraculous healing powers my sister thought they would in covering up the evidence that something was not right when I was presented to my mother. When our mother saw me and the condition, I was in I recall that we both got a good telling off; my sister for being so wicked towards me, and me for being so stupid believing what she was saying!

A BICYCLE NOT MADE FOR TWO

After my first meeting with Margaret things started to settle for me, although I did have the odd occasion where I would be lying in bed and something would come into the room. The breathing would start, or a slow long hissing sound would develop.

I learnt very quickly about being able to control my thoughts and some of the things I would hear. Of course, Margaret would pop in every now and then as a gentle reminder that I was not alone.

I'm going to jump a few years to my teenage years; a time of strange happenings within a young person's body, not only hormonal changes but development of the psychic mind.

Puberty is a time when a psychic's or spirit medium's powers become heightened; a time when they become more vulnerable to spirit attack.

It was at this time that I was given a bike from a family friend. The bike was probably the same age as me, twelve. It was a chopper bike from the seventies. I really thought I was the bees' knees with my little gear stick and extended saddle. I was the King of the Road!

It had not struck me that the bike belonged to their oldest son who had been killed in a car accident several years ago.

Living in a country village there were plenty of woodlands and paths to go cycling. During this period of my childhood, I was out all the time on my chopper. One warm night I had gone for a ride up to the Barnett Hill woods. As I was peddling down the path that ran parallel to the woods, I heard Margaret's voice in my head.

'Joseph, get home quickly something terrible is going to happen to you'. It all happened so quickly. Margaret's voice made me brake hard. I stopped and placed both feet firmly on the ground. I began to feel a cold sensation running up my spine.

I then started to feel a tight grip around my waist as if I was carrying a passenger on the bike. 'This is my bike not yours' the icy voice shouted in my ear. In fear I fell off the bike and clambered to my feet. I looked over towards the bike. There was no one there, just the chopper lying on its side.

I could feel that same chilled feeling come over me, at my side. Margaret appeared, 'behind you!' she shouted. I turned sharply and in front of me 10 feet or so away stood the owner of the bike, in adult form. He stood staring at me. His body had a tear through the middle of it. It looked as if someone had chopped the top of his head with an axe.

'This is my bike, not yours' he shouted. Blood appeared to be trickling from his face. I could even make out parts of his brain dripping down his left cheek.

The feelings I was experiencing did not seem right. Why would someone I knew be appearing to me this way? And why would he make me feel so scared? Margaret yanked my arm 'this is not who you think it is. This is an evil entity that has attached itself to the emotions of the bike. RUN!'

I turned and ran. I could feel that the entity was following closely behind. I did somehow manage to pick up the bike and run. However, as I bent down to pick the bike up I felt a strange burning sensation on my shoulder. I continued to run down the road until I came to the farm. Running through the open gate I dropped the bike in the garden and ran into the house.

I felt safe but scared. The burning sensation was now throbbing on my shoulder. Going into the bathroom to check it out, I could see what appeared to look like teeth marks. Margaret appeared and I could see her standing behind me in the mirror. 'That was a lucky escape' she said. 'Congratulations, you have experienced your first entity attack!'

That experience gave me the uneasy feeling that I was no longer safe, and that I could no longer be complacent. I had begun to realise that Margaret could only warn me, not protect me against entities.

It's sad, but I could no longer face playing on my chopper again after that experience, so it was put away at the back of one of the old sheds on the farm.

That night Margaret appeared in my room. Sitting on the corner of my bed she explained that sometimes entities pick up on very strong negative feeling. They attach themselves to items that are involved with heightened emotions. They could then lie dormant until something awakens them. She told me that an entity can appear as dead loved ones and mislead people into feeling a false sense of security. These entities would then slowly drain the person until they were totally reliant upon then. Making them spiritually weak, it would be at this point the entity would then take possession of the person causing them to do terrible things to themselves and others.

'You're buggered if that happens!' said Margaret. 'You then need an exorcism, which is not guaranteed to work'. You would be right to guess that I did not sleep well that night.

On a positive note, I did receive a new bike from my best friend Jack after his mum had brought him a new one. Again, I was King of the Road.

Jack too would come to experience some of the supernatural goings on, poor lad. He still kept coming round and spending weekends with me at the farm. Jack was the one person whom I could talk to; he was the one person who believed me when others did not.

There would be times that the spirits would risk exposing themselves to Jack in order to frighten him away however, they never did, and I'm grateful for that

THE POSSESSION OF THE EVIL ARMCHAIR

It was shortly after the incident with the chopper that my mother got a part-time job cleaning for a local elderly lady, in a big house with lots of old furniture.

One day she brought back an old wooden armchair which she decided would go nicely in my bedroom. I was happy with this, as it would fit in well with all the other second-hand furniture I had acquired.

I recall that I was lying in bed watching a video when over the sound of the television a loud breathing noise started. I got up to turn the sound down and while turning the sound down, I noticed that there was a dark figure sitting in the armchair that was situated in the corner of the room.

Shocked, I fell back onto the bed. The figure did not move; it just sat there. The figure had no facial expression or any distinctive features, just a dark figure of a large man.

I could sense that this was not the normal visit from a spirit and by the darkness that surrounded him I was aware that the spirit was not human.

'What is it you want?', I quietly asked. There was no reply. I asked again 'What do you want?' Again, there was no reply. I started to get anxious. 'Margaret, where are you?' I thought as I continued to focus on the shadow man.

Margaret appeared in the corner of the bedroom, looked over to the chair and then looked back at me, 'it's a shadow demon, a dark spirit which is evil to the core, a tormentor of souls'.

'What do I do?' I asked. 'Nothing' she replied, 'you do not have the skills to get rid of it and all I can do is help to protect you from it; but it is stronger than me.'

Now I was afraid. I closed my eyes and tried to concentrate on making the shadow demon disappear. Opening my eyes, the demon was still there. The shadow turned and even though it had no facial features, I knew it was staring at me, a faint hissing sound emitting from him.

Margaret came over to me 'all we can do is ride this out. If it was going to hurt you it would have done so by now'. I was so confused. What on Earth did it want? Why did it not communicate with me?

'All you could do', Margaret said 'is to get into bed and try to ignore it'. I got into bed and closed my eyes. Even though I had my eyes closed I could feel that this demon was still sitting in the armchair staring at me.

When morning came, I opened my eyes, and the shadow demon was gone. I felt exhausted and even though I had slept I was tired and drained. The following night the demon was there again, silent but staring at me. I lay in bed watching it thinking to myself that even if I told my parents, they would not believe me.

Lying there in my bed, my eyes closed I started to see images in my mind; horrible images of people dying, people who I knew. It was terrifying. Some deaths were natural some were horrific.

I saw a young boy being buried in a wood. He had been abducted while on his paper round. His body lying rotting in the leaves, finger marks around his neck where he had been strangled.

These sorts of visions had never happened before. I woke myself up in fear. Looking over to the chair I could see the demon still sitting there but this time I could make out he had features, sharp piercing red eyes, and hollow grey mouth.

Seeing his features made me more fearful. 'Leave me alone' I shouted, 'leave me alone'. It was at this point that the demon communicated; it laughed in a deep and low tone.

The demon looked at me and started to talk in a language I could not understand. He was not loud. but I could still make out that he was chanting at me. I turned over to face the wall. I tried with all my might to block out the sound of his chants, but it did not work. I could still hear the same constant chant again and again turning like a wheel in my head.

Several times during the night I would turn and face the demon pleading for him to stop, but it was to no avail.

As morning came the shadow demon had gone, and I finally had peace in my mind. However, the disturbed night had taken its toll on my physical and emotional wellbeing. This continued cyclically for some days.

On the fourth day I called upon Margaret to come and help me. 'Please help' me I kept calling, but she would not appear. I felt lost and alone, no one to talk to no one to ask for help. I was desperate. I did not want to spend another night listening to the shadow demon chanting his evil verses at me.

It was around 7pm that night whilst I was watching television with my parents that Margaret appeared to me. Standing in front of me she whispered, 'come into the dining room, I have some information for you'. I followed her discreetly to the dining room.

'Take a pen and paper and write down the following verses by word'.

> *'Lord Jesus, in Your Holy Name, I bind all evil spirits of the air, water, ground, underground, and netherworld. I further bind, in Jesus' name, any and all emissaries of the satanic headquarters and claim the Precious Blood of Jesus on the air, atmosphere, water, ground and their fruits around us, the underground and the netherworld below.*
>
> *Heavenly Father, allow Your Son Jesus to come now with the Holy Spirit, the Blessed Virgin Mary, the holy angels and the saints to protect me from all harm and to keep all evil spirits from taking revenge on me in any way.*

'Repeat this three times'

> *In The Holy Name of Jesus, I seal myself, my relatives, this room, and all sources of supply in the Precious Blood of Jesus Christ.*

She continued, telling me to repeat the following paragraph three times:

> *'In the Holy Name of Jesus, I break and dissolve any and all curses, hexes, spells, snares, traps, lies, obstacles, deceptions, diversions, spiritual influences, evil wishes, evil desires, hereditary seals, known and unknown, and every dysfunction and disease from any source including my mistakes and sins. In Jesus' Name, I sever the transmission of any and all satanic vows,*

pacts, spiritual bonds, soul ties, and satanic works.

In Jesus' Name, I break and dissolve any and all links and effects of links and of all sorts, and any form of worship that does not offer true honour to Jesus Christ.

Holy Spirit, please reveal to me through word of knowledge any evil spirits that have attached themselves to me in any way.'

In the name of Jesus, I rebuke you spirit of Satan. I command to go directly to Jesus, without manifestation and without harm to me or anyone, so that He can dispose of you according to His Holy Will.

I thank You, Heavenly Father for Your Love. I thank You, Holy Spirit for *empowering me to be aggressive against Satan and evil spirits. I thank You, Jesus, for setting me free. I thank You, Mary, for interceding for me with the holy angels and the saints.*

Lord Jesus, fill me with charity, compassion, faith, gentleness, hope, humility, joy, kindness, light, love, mercy, modesty, patience, peace, purity, security, tranquillity, trust, truth, understanding, and wisdom.

Help me to walk in Your light and truth, illuminated by the Holy Spirit so that together we may praise, honour, and glorify Our Father in time and in eternity. For You, Lord Jesus, are, 'the way, the truth, and the life' and you 'have come that we might have life and have it more abundantly.

Evil spirit be gone. Evil spirit be gone. Evil spirit be gone.'

'Now when the shadow demon appears again chant this back at him and you should be able to overpower him. It is an old Catholic banishing prayer, and this should work, but you must believe that the words are power, and this power will drive spirits out and really kick some evil butts!'

Due to the nature of the prayer and the sensitivity of the words I have omitted some verses out for the protection of the reader.

With apprehension I read and re-read the verses trying to make the words flow freely in my mind. I was so scared; I had no idea how this demon would react. Would it go easily, or would it put up a fight?

Little did I know at this point that Margaret was preparing me for events which would recur for many years.

That night I went to bed early firstly due to wanting to try out my verses and secondly, I was so exhausted through lack of sleep. I folded the paper with the verses on and kept it very tightly in my hand, too frightened to let it go.

I undressed and slipped into my pyjamas. placed my pillows up against the wall and sat up in bed waiting for the shadow demon to appear. For an hour I waited and still no shadow demon appeared.

I turned on the television for some mindless night-time viewing, occasionally looking over at the chair, however nothing appeared. In one way I was disappointed but in another, I was relieved. Maybe I was going to be able to sleep well this night!

Turning the television off I settled the pillows correctly on the bed. I lay down facing the wall and started to drift asleep; It did not take me long. I had barely closed my eyes before I was asleep.

It was not long before I could feel something heavy pressing down on my chest; a tight feeling grasping at my chest as if I was gasping for breath. I opened my eyes and floating around a foot above me was the shadow demon with his piercing red eye glaring down into mine.

I was trapped. I could not move. My whole body was paralysed. It was then that Margaret appeared looking as if she was trying to pull the shadow demon off me. 'The verses' she screamed 'read the verses'.

The shadow demon looked in the direction where Margaret was screaming. He swiped her with his left arm. Margaret disappeared.

This gave me enough time to roll over and grab the verses from under my pillow. Turning the lamp on, I sat upright and started to read the verses very slowly and quietly. The shadow demon paused what he was doing and hissed violently.

'Foolish boy' he said with a grizzly voice 'do you really think you can banish me?' he stared into my eyes. The more he stared the redder his eyes became.

I continued reading, following the instructions Margaret had earlier told me. I was terrified, but as I read, the shadow demon started to step backward, shouting, and hissing back at me, 'stupid boy you have no power over me'.

'I will destroy your family; I will rip their heads off and spit into their souls' I continued reading the verses with a sense of inner strength, focusing on the words that I had before me.

Again and again, the shadow demon hissed and shouted back at me. I could feel he was getting weaker and weaker. He looked as if he was going to sink back into the armchair.

I paused for just one second to take a breath; it was at this point that I felt a sharp stinging pain across my face. The shadow demon had lashed out at me and scratched my face. The pain gave me a burning sensation. I quickly began repeating the verses. The shadow demon again started to shout his threat towards me, threatening my friends and family. After around 5 minutes the shadow demon had vanished into the armchair.

It is strange to say but sitting there on my bed after forcing away a shadow demon I felt immensely proud of myself. I looked up and in the corner of the room Margaret stood smiling.

'Well done' she said, 'you did well, however he will be back. These demons are tormentors and are strong. He will gather his energy and return'.

'What do I do?' I asked. 'There is nothing you can do', she said, 'All you can do is prepare yourself and make sure that a shadow demon does not catch you un-aware. I will warn you if I can'.

It was at this moment that I started to realise that I would never be safe again.

I went down the stairs to the bathroom to see what marks I had on my face. Looking in the mirror I could see 3 long scratches running down the right side of my face. I was shocked.

I returned upstairs to bed. I did not feel comfortable with the chair in my room, so picking it up I placed on the landing.

The next morning my mother wanted to know why I had put the chair on the landing and why I had scratched my face. I tried explaining about the shadow demon and that it had scratched me in a fit of rage. She did not respond with any comments or give me the usual response of 'it's your over-active imagination'.

I did not know what to do now. All that was in my mind was wondering what would happen if the shadow demon came back. What happens if there is more than one?

It just happened that during the day one of the church elders had paid us a visit. As I was close to him and had a good relationship with him, I decided to tell him what had happened.

To my surprise he believed me; his explanation was that the devil and his demons can possess certain items, including furniture. He said that the chair was likely to be possessed by a demon. The demon would stay attached to the chair and will attack and torment anyone that was sensitive. He could not explain how spirits possess items. I later learnt that it was not difficult for them to possess items as all they needed was a channel, or doorway for them to enter our lives.

He suggested to my mum that we take the chair into the garden and burn it; only then would the demon go and not come back.

Again, I would learn that this was not entirely correct; all this would do would be get rid of the item. The demon itself would still be there. You also need to put in preventive measures to stop the demon from returning.

However, I did not need to be told twice, I ran up the stairs and brought the armchair down. I placed it in the garden. I grabbed a box of matches out of the kitchen cupboard and then took great pleasure in lighting the cushions, watching it all burn.

That night going to bed, I was confident that I had dealt with the shadow demon; that I would finally have a good night's sleep.

As I lay in bed Margaret appeared to me in the middle of the room, 'you did the right thing getting rid of the chair' she commented 'however the shadow demon will come back. Not when you expect it; it could be months or even years'.

She explained that now the chair was gone the demon would wait and then possess something else; it was just a matter of time.

She taught me that demons filled vacuums in our lives when we were at our lowest and feel empty. She explained that the only way to stop them was to fill our lives with positive things.

Margaret telling me this did not make me feel good, however I felt that at long as I was starting to learn new things and was beginning to feel that there was hope, I could deal with what was happening in my world.

I got into bed turned my head to the wall pulled the blankets over me, closed my eyes, and slept well.

NEVER TO CATCH THAT TRAIN

You may hear people say that the dead can't hurt you and that it is the living you should be worried about. I beg to differ! This next story haunts me to this day and taught me that the dead can really harm you if they are twisted and evil enough to gain the power to do so.

I would have been around 14 years old and had been into town on the train to meet my friend Jack. As I was sitting at the station waiting for the train to arrive, I noticed that there was a man in a suit standing at the edge of the platform. He looked as if he obviously worked in town and commuted to work on the train.

As I was sitting there, I could feel this strange feeling come over me. I can only describe it as the feeling you get when you haven't eaten, and your blood sugars are low. The shivers started to take over me and everything went hazy, as if I was going into some kind of trance. My vison went very blurry as if I was looking under water.

I turned to my right, and it was at that moment I saw the figure of a cloaked man around the age of 40, dressed in period clothes from around the time of Guy Fawkes. He stared at me and laughed. I could tell that this was a human spirit and not an evil demon or entity.

The spirit was standing right behind the man in the suit. I watched, powerless as I heard the announcement that the high-speed train to Birmingham was coming through the station and that everyone should stand back from the platform.

I could hear the sound of the train speeding towards the station, the noise of the horn in the distance. It was in the split of a second that the spirit had raised his hands and pushed the man in the suit straight into the path of the oncoming train. He did not stand a chance. His body was pulled under the front of the train as his leg, head and arm detached from his body. I screamed as I heard the screeching of the brakes and jolted back hard against my seat. I heard the voice of Margaret telling me to open my eyes. As I opened my eyes the man in the suit was still standing there. "You had a vison", she said. "The man standing over there is marked for death. The spirits see him and eventually they will get him. Always remember those who are bad and evil while alive take it with them when they die".

It was a couple of weeks after that vison, that I saw in the local paper a family man had committed suicide by throwing himself under a train. The article explained that there had been no indications from him that anything was wrong and that it was totally out of character.

The picture in the article was the man in the suit. Was my vision a glimpse of the future? I can't say for sure but through my experience I know that spirits can be dangerous, so always keep this in mind and be respectful.

LUCY IN THE WARDROBE, WITHOUT DIAMONDS

After my experience with the shadow demon, I decided that I would do more research and trying to learn more about spirits and the occult.

Being a teenager, I must have seemed a bit strange sitting in the local library reading books on exorcism and ghosts experiences. I found a book by a famous medium which gave lots of explanations as to what was going on in my own life.

Key things I learnt would help forge my life from an early age. I began to understand that we are all born with certain gifts; some people are fantastic artists painting wonderful landscapes and masterpieces, some are gifted with being bilingual, and others are able to solve mathematical problems with ease. In mine and others' cases, I could see and communicate with spirits, but also see into the future.

Margaret visited me regularly after the experience with the shadow demon, giving me needed reassurance that I was going to be ok. Very little had happened weeks after the armchair incident. This period of relative calm was, however, to be short-lived.

It was a particular frosty night. Having very ineffective central heating in the house, I remember going to bed cold. I lay in bed enjoying reading a Famous Five book when I started to hear a whispering sound coming from where my wardrobe was situated.

I looked up from my book and stared hard in the direction of where the whispering was coming from. As I focused on the wardrobe. the door slowly started to open; just enough for me to be able to see inside.

I was starting to get really nervous now, expecting something terrible to jump out and grab me. I held my breath, ready to duck under the blankets.

The whispering continued for a few seconds until I could make out a small face peering through the open door. The face was that of a small girl with long curly brown hair. She looked around 9 years old. I asked her who she was and what she wanted. She whispered that she was scared and lost and could not find her mummy. The whisper turned into a cry, 'I can't find my mummy I can't find my mummy', she cried.

I asked her what her name was. She replied telling me it was Lucy. Stupidly, I asked her what she was doing in the wardrobe. She replied that she did not know where she was and repeated that she was looking for her mummy.

I called out to Margaret for help. Margaret appeared to me and looked over at the little girl. 'It's a lost spirit' she said 'it's trapped here on this plane. She probably doesn't realise she is dead. You are going to have to convince her that she should cross over'. I looked over to Margaret to ask her how but she had gone.

I looked back over at Lucy, 'what's happened to you and what can you remember?'. She told me that she had gone into the fields to find her mother who was out working the land. On the way this man had approached her and had taken her, dragging her into the woods. She continued to tell me that she remembered his big hand squeezing her neck and everything going blank. She said no more, but just stared at me, crying.

It occurred to me that she had been murdered. How on earth am I going to help her? As I focused more, I could clearly see black marks around her throat. My mind went dark. I can only explain what I saw next as being as though I was watching a television programme, in my mind.

I could clearly see Lucy walking down a pathway, next to a wood; it was a vivid vision. as if I was standing there watching her.

I could see the man following behind her, fidgeting with his hands as he got closer and closer, his eyes dark, his face twisted. I could tell that they were from the Victorian era by the way they were dressed.

He caught up with her and grabbed her hand and dragged her away into the woods like she was a small rag doll. I was powerless. I could not move or speak. I seemed to be floating as I followed them into the woods.

The stranger was now sitting on top of Lucy, slowly squeezing the life from her body as he strangled her with his huge hand. He laughed as the last breaths of life drained from her.

After he released his grip, her head flopped to the side> Her shocked, scared and staring eyes remaining open even though she was dead.

The shock of watching this cold-blooded murder shook me out of my vision. I regained a focus on Lucy looking at her. Clearly, she was still distressed.

'I'm sorry Lucy I have to tell you that something terrible happened to you and you are dead'. There was no other way I could explain her situation.

'I want my mummy', she cried. 'I'm sure your mummy is looking for you' I answered. 'Are you able to see any lights?' I asked her.

'Yes', she replied, 'but the voice tells me not to go into the light because that's where the bad man is'. I looked her straight in the face. All of my instincts were telling me that she needed to cross over into the light. This is also what one of the books I had read had suggested.

'No Lucy, you must go into the light. The voice is the bad man who wants to keep you in the darkness. Your mummy is in the light. Go now; run into the light'.

Her face disappeared and I could sense she was heading into the light. I felt a sense of achievement. I felt pleased and proud of myself.

I rolled over and faced the wall still feeling chuffed. I closed my eyes and yawned. As I breathed out, I heard the creaking hinges of the wardrobe door open once more. I turned thinking it was Lucy coming back. I opened my eyes but this time it was not Lucy's face I saw. It was not the face of a child, but the face that looked like it was half goat half man. It was high up in the open door of the wardrobe. Its body was completely covered with hair, and it had hoofed feet. I was terrified. I could not move I was frozen with fear. It was not the same fear as I had felt when faced with the shadow demon; this was a fear far deeper.

The creature looked me in the eyes and a dark voice inside my head boomed 'the child was mine! You will pay for what you have done. I will make you suffer beyond what your feeble mind will cope with'. I closed my eyes and tried to focus on switching off from what I could hear inside my head.

There was silence, I opened my eyes and there stood Albert, whom I had not seen since I was six.

'Oh dear' Albert said. 'Joseph, you have crossed a line. You have taken a soul from an evil being. The thing you saw was a demon from the beginning; from a time when there were no humans on the earth. These demons have been here since the dawn of time'.

I could feel a dread building inside me. 'These demons feed on the bad things that happen to people, the negative energies that misery and pain cause. This demon will not kill but, it will try to torment you and turn you mind inside out. These are the demons that turn people insane. However, I will protect you and prevent it from turning you, but you also need to be strong and block it from attacking your mind'.

Albert had disappeared and peace came to my room yet again. I felt uneasy and unsettled. My mind now was filled with terror and dread. At least I knew Lucy was at peace even if I was not.

TO INSANITY AND BEYOND

How does a teenager entering young manhood cope mentally with everything that was happening to him and the visions and visits he was receiving from the spirit world?

I had seen things that you would find hard to comprehend; I had been attacked, threatened and dragged into a world of experiences and visons I did not want.

I entered a very painful part of my life that I talk very little about, however it is important to share this experience with you. It is important that you understand that mental health problems can't always be explained and no matter how much medication is given, not all voices disappear.

Please remember that cases like mine and others like me are rare and if there is a genuine mental health problem professional help must be taken.

The experience of the demon in the wardrobe played on my mind for many days after; I would go to bed at night and close my eyes and all I would hear would be the wardrobe door opening.

I would roll over and look over at the open door. I would not see anything there, but the voices would start, constantly speaking telling me that I was in danger. The voices would tell me that I was going to die, that the spirits would get me and that there would nothing anyone, or I could do to save me.

This would go on and on constantly in my head over and over again. I tried with all my might to concentrate on other thoughts, hoping that the demonic voices would stop.

I tried putting earphones on to play music through my cassette player. This only slightly drowned out the sound of the voices.

Due to lack of sleep my mental health was being affected. I started to suffer from mood swings. Feelings of depression and loneliness started to appear. My parents were starting to worry. 'I'm going to take you to the doctor, and he can sort you out', my mother suggested. So off to the doctor I went.

As I sat there in the doctor's room, he looked over at me with an extremely judgemental eye; 'your mother tells me you have been having a few issues with sleep and hearing voices'. 'Yes', I answered and went on to explain everything that had gone on with the demons and Lucy in the wardrobe, foolishly thinking he was going to help and support me.

Every now and then the doctor would look up from his notes and give me a blank stare. Looking back as an adult he must have thought I was one hell of a loopy kid!

After the consultation, he decided that anti-depressants would cure me of my problems and a visit to a psychologist at the hospital would also be helpful.

So, as a good boy, I took the medication the doctor had suggested would it make me better. Would it stop the voices? Would the spirits disappear? No, the medication's effect on me made things worse. I began to feel depressed, low, and angry; the medication was having a reverse effect.

Due to the constant voice emitting from the wardrobe, and to the total exhaustion caused by the medication, I was going deteriorating rapidly. To me, it was obvious that the medication was not working.

Margaret was still about, appearing every night to check up on me and to try to help put things in perspective. She sat on the bed and started to help me focus on my powers of thought. She started to teach me to focus, 'now think of a safe place', she would suggest. 'Imagine that you are in a room where you are in control of the thickness of the walls around you. Imagine that when the demon's voice speaks the walls of the room get thicker and thicker, until you can no longer hear the voice. This will help you to shut out any of the voices from the unwanted spirits and entities, and it will protect you from any mind attack'.

I practised this technique for the next few days, imagining the wall around me being built high above slowly getting thicker and thicker until the voice disappeared.

To my relief it was starting to work. Day by day the voice got light and lighter until it finally disappeared. I had successfully learnt the skill of blocking. Margaret was right, it worked.

Being able to sleep peacefully at night was great. As soon as the demon spirit had realised that its attack was no longer having the desired effect, it stopped appearing in the wardrobe and attacking me with its evil voices.

A week or so after learning to control the voices, an appointment to see the psychologist at D block in Kidderminster arrived. Hesitantly, I accompanied my mother and father to the appointment.

Arriving at the hospital I was worried about what was going to happen. I had seen the films about mental asylums and the awful things that happens to those who go there.

I had visions of being wired up to electric shock machines and having numerous amounts of volts going through my head and body, causing me to pee myself.

Stricken with panic I hesitated. 'Come on then' my mother said, 'let's get this over with'. I continued to walk down the corridor. To my relief Margaret appeared beside me.

'Don't worry' she said grinning 'I've got this all in-hand. You just listen to me and say exactly what I tell you to say, and this will be over and done with in no time!''.

Sitting in the waiting area we waited for the nurse to come out and tell us when it was our turn to go in.

'Would you like your mother to come in with you or are you ok?' she asked, directing us into the room. 'I'm happy to go on my own', I replied.

Stepping into the office the psychologist was sitting at the side of his desk, a 60 something year-old man, bearded and half-moon glasses.

'Sit down Joseph. I'm Mr Van der Linden' he said pointing to a small armchair. 'Your general practitioner informs me that you have been hearing voices. Could you tell me more about this?'.

I thought for a second and contemplated what to say. 'Wait for it' Margaret said, 'they're nearly here' 'Well what have you got to say?' Mr Van der Linden repeated as I sat silently.

'They're here' Margaret shouted, 'look behind him'. I looked up and yes, there was a woman and a man standing behind Mr Van der Linden. I would say they were in their late 30 dressed in 1930 – 40s clothes.

'Good afternoon' they said, speaking in a strange voice. 'We are Fredrick's parents'. 'It's ok', Margaret said 'even though they are speaking in a foreign language you will understand in your mind what they are saying'.

'I can see dead people' I answered looking straight at Mr Van der Linden. 'That is what is wrong with me; I see and hear spirits'.

'Ok interesting', Mr Van der Linden answered. 'How long has this been going on for?'

I felt a sense of confidence filling inside me; a confidence I had not felt before. I felt as if I was now finally in control. 'I was about 6 years old when I first saw the spirits and it's been going on since then, I guess'.

'And what do these spirits tell you?' he asked, looking down at me, eyes peering over the rim of his glasses.

'Well, some of the spirits tell me how they died, some of them are trying to connect with their family members and others are evil spirits, who simply want to hurt and possess people'.

I continued to stare at Mr Van der Linden straight in his eye as I explained what life had been like. I could tell straight away that he did not believe me. His look of disbelief was written across his face. I knew instantly that he thought, "here we go another nut case!"

'This is very much make-believe' he said, 'Do you really expect me to believe that there are dead people all around us? This appears to be a case of delusion young man, probably the result of too much teenage hormones running wild around your body. What you need is a short stay here on D block for some psychiatric treatments. That will help take away all these silly thoughts and feelings'.

'Yes', I answered, 'I do expect you to believe me, and there is no way I'm staying here. In fact, we have your mother and father here with us'.

'Really' Mr Van der Linden said with a slight smirk on his face.

'Let's wipe that smirk off his face' Margaret said, grinning 'ask his parents what message they have for him'.

I turned to the couple that were standing at his side 'what message do you have for me?'

His mother came forward 'tell our son our names and that we died during the war. We had managed to get Fredrick Junior out of Germany when he was just a baby. My sister managed to smuggle him out, but we were caught at the border and then taken to the camp. My husband and I were separated and that was the last we both saw of each other alive. Even in spirit my husband is still traumatised by the events of our deaths. My sister's name was Rebecca and she brought him over to England and settled her with her husband Tom. They brought Fredrick up as their own. Can you tell him we both love him and our names our Fredrick and Hanna'. As I took in all the information, I could not help but notice and feel the aura of sadness that surrounded this couple. As I looked over at Mr Van der Linden, I noticed the couple had now gone back over to the other side (I will discuss the other side later).

"Right let's wrap this up" I said smiling. "Now, Mr Van der Linden, I have just had your mother and father, Hanna and Fredrick, here with us. They have told me all about your mother's sister Rebecca escaping to England during the war and bringing you up with her husband and how your mother and father then died in a German camp'.

Mr Van der Linden sat mouth open. "How? How can you know that?', he said in a slight stutter.

'Now do you believe me?' I asked in a more confident and determined voice.

Mr Van der Linden looked back at me, his face pale and shocked. 'I don't know what to say' he mumbled. 'I think we had better end our session'.

'There you go sunshine' Margaret whispered, 'that's taught him a lesson he won't forget in a hurry'.

Mr Van der Linden stood up and quickly ushered me to the door where my parents were eagerly waiting his verdict.

'Erm after our discussion, I feel in my professional opinion that there is nothing wrong with your son, just an over-active imagination that's all, no signs of mental health. Thank you and goodbye'.

Driving home I felt a sense of relief and calm. I felt that I had won a small victory and Margaret was to thank. My parents did not utter a word during the drive home, slipping slowly back into their strange world of denial.

THERE'S SOMETHING DEAD IN THE GRAVEYARD

After my experience with the child psychologist, I made a concerted effort to keep it low-key when it came to talking to dead people. Summer school holidays were spent with my best friend from the village. We had known each other for years.

Many evenings were spent at her house watching the latest horror film on Betamax. For those who are puzzled, Betamax were the film tapes before VHS and DVDs.

Anyway, getting back to the story, watching the latest horror was the highlight of my week; from the Amityville Horror to Freddy Krueger, I could not get enough of them, even if they scared the wits out of me! Could you image if horror films like The Conjuring were out back then? I think I would have passed out!

Unfortunately, after watching these films, I would have to walk home in the dark alone, passing a few fields and hedges on the way. So, you can imagine knowing what I could see It was always an adrenaline filled run up the road.

It was on one particular night that we had watched an especially scary supernatural style film where I started to walk home. My heart was pounding, and my mind was trying to focus on anything non scary. However, that was not going to be the case. As I walked along the pavement, the clouded sky blocking out the moon light, I had a sense of fear and nervousness I had not felt before.

I felt a coldness rise up my spine and a tight feeling pressing upon my chest. I knew something was terribly wrong.

As I speeded up my walk, I could feel that there was a presence behind me. This was a presence that I had never felt before; a presence that made my legs feel as if they were sticking to the pavement. I knew then that I was rooted to the ground; I could not move. I was left standing still like a human statue.

Where the hell was Margaret? Where was Albert? They were nowhere to be felt. I thought of the special words I had used before in the past, but try as I might, the words would not leave my mouth.

I was frozen and alone. The feeling of pain and tightness in my chest began to increase up to the point it felt like my skin was turning inside out.

Closing my eyes, I tried to re-focus the power to resist whatever it was that was attacking me. I could not focus. I kept thinking, 'Margaret, help me!'. It was at this point that I could see what it was that was penetrating my body.

Before me was a dark and grey man-like figure with no hair, just dark leathery skin, long crooked hands, and fingers which were pushing themselves into my chest. Looking into its eye I could see that they were a fiery yellow.

I could hear a piercing screaming sound penetrating into the centre of my brain. As it pushed itself into me, I could see images of an awful dimension; bodies littering the ground, the charred bodies of babies and children, adults hanging from trees, bodies that were burnt to a crisp, fire burning up from the earth.

It was a picture of what I would imagine hell to look like. I was terrified. I was now looking into the mind of this creature, connected as one as it entered my body.

I lost all sense of consciousness. I was totally under the control of this being. I am unaware of the time scale that had passed but the next thing I remember was lying on my back looking up at the darkened sky with the shape of a stone cross above me. It was now that I realised that I was in the village graveyard, lying on one the graves.

I had no recollection of how I had got there. Sitting up, I could see the evil figure looking at me with its fiery eyes. 'I could kill you now', it hissed, 'but what would be the point of that? I am the eater of souls and the killer of children'.

I was terrified. I wanted it to be a bad dream. I wanted to wake up and think 'phew thank God that's over'. But that was not going to happen; this was real.

The creature started to speak again 'Everything you know about the spirit world is nothing compared to the reality of what is on the other side. There is no Heaven, no Hell just a void of what you are. You take what you are over with you. Like me, not everything is human. I am the creation of something older and a lot more sinister.'

'What are you?' I demanded 'Where is Margaret?'. 'That whore?' he hissed back at me. 'She is from the Human realm and has no hold over me'.

I asked the creature what it wanted with me. 'I will use you for things that I want you to do' it replied, 'You will see me again and you will do as I ask'.

Terrified, I tried not to answer or show emotion. I felt that this was something that could hurt me and cause me internal harm; I felt vulnerable for the first time in years.

I closed my eyes and started praying, 'I wouldn't waste my time!' it said, 'I'm far older than any Christian belief'.

Everything I believed had now started to fall apart. All of the faith in a higher being had slipped away. Reality was hitting me like a thump on the jaw.

I opened my eyes and the creature with the yellow eyes had gone; disappeared as quickly as it appeared and took over my body.

Sitting alone in the graveyard alone and frightened I felt threatened and lost. 'Sorry I'm late'. Looking up there was Margaret. 'Sorry I could not get to you; I did try' she said. 'That was a demon from the darkness; something that does not have a soul; something so twisted and evil it is more like a parasite, possessing and draining the human spirit until there is nothing left.'

'Neither Albert nor I can help you when it comes to these types of demons. Again, all you can do is fight against it and find some way of stopping the possession. It feeds off fear'.

'Well, you can say that again! It had a whole feast of me, I was petrified', I replied. Building up a resistance would be the only way I could defend myself from the demon,

'What does it want with me?', I asked. 'To possess you and make you do things you don't want to do. So many times these demons possess people and make them do the most inhumane things to others. They can even make a person jump in front of a train. That's how powerful they are; they are not to be taken lightly'.

'My advice for you would be to train your mind not to be vulnerable to fear. Be aware that there are things out in the other realms that can kill you and others. Become a soldier for the light and fight against these creatures. Read and learn all you can to equip you with the right tools to fight.'

'This demon has you in its sights and will be back. Now that it knows you know it exists, it will come back for you; maybe not now, but in time'.

'Well, thank you Margaret! I don't think I will ever sleep again! Remind me to come to you again when I need reassurance!'.

Looking back now, it was at this point that I realised that the true reason for my ability had been set out in front of me. I had come to the point where in my head I had been given the answer to 'why me?'. Everything that I had experienced when it came to the spirit realm would lead me to this. The demon had left me with questions, I had never really questioned before.

Was there a God? Did Jesus exist? Are there angels? Is there a Heaven and a Hell, or do we just cross over to a different realm?

I asked Margaret these questions and all she replied was that,

'All I know is what I know! I see what I see and can do what I can do; every spirit that is human is different. Some cross over peacefully and watch over their loved ones. Some can't accept they are dead and are tormented by a non-reality and then you have the bad ones.

That's all I can say. It is up to you to learn your own path.'

This is the first time I have ever spoken about this experience.

THE PATHWAY TO ENLIGHTENMENT

Thinking back to the experience of my first possession, it was at this time that I started to research and become obsessed with the different realms of spirit and demonology.

Before the invention of the internet, we had great centres of research called libraries. It was at the library that I would sit for hours reading books on the occult, on theology and demon possession.

From horror novels to religious texts, I was on a mission to absorb all the information I could. I recall watching one of those exorcist films where a priest proclaimed that in order to fight your enemy, you need to know who your enemy is.

I would search the yellow pages looking for independent book shops and save my money to buy the second-hand books containing rites of rituals and manuscripts of possession.

I made every concerted effect to conceal my obsession with learning from my parents. Their religious ideology was against every form of communication with spirit.

'What's that you're reading?' Margaret asked as she appeared to me, up in my bedroom. 'The 16th Century Witch Hunter', I replied.

Looking over at Margaret I noticed that there was a sad look upon her face. 'What's up with you?', I asked.

'Nothing', she replied. 'Is it interesting?' she asked. 'Yes', I answered 'it's about some guy who goes around villages hunting witches and devil worshipers.'

'Sounds like the story of my life', she mumbled.

I looked up again at her, visible only to my eyes. Her shape perfectly fixed in my mind. In all the years that she had been appearing to me, this was the first time that I saw emotion reflected in her face.

She moved over to me and placed her spirit hands over my eyes.

'Take a deep breath and open your mind' she whispered, 'allow me to show you a glimpse into the past'. I closed my eyes and started the experience. As a child I had often felt the sensation of slipping into a deep sleep, whilst remaining conscious of everything that is going on around me. Margaret was showing me how to travel into the psychic past.

In the vision I could see a human fleshly non-dead Margaret in a Tudor style house cooking in the kitchen; she appeared happy and oblivious to my presence in the house.

Here I was the spirit, and she was the living person. To my surprise she seemed so happy and content, working away in her small kitchen humming a tune as she pressed hard into her mortar and pestle grinding up her herbs. It gave me a calm sense of serenity and peace watching her working away with all her herbs hanging all around her from string attached to the low ceiling. I had never thought of Margaret having a life of her own; being a real person with feelings and a family.

A sudden bang on the door startled my attention. I looked over to the door where two men in black cloaks burst through the door, 'Margaret Bunt! Under the order of Mathew Hopkins, you are charged with the crimes of witchcraft. You are to come with us now'. Before Margaret could flee to the side door another two men burst through the door. The man on the left raised a large wooden club striking Margaret on the side of the head. With this one blow Margaret fell, hitting the stone floor hard with a trickle of blood now pouring from her temple. I was powerless to help her as the two men proceeded to drag her out of the door. They roughly bundled her into the back of a cart.

I felt sick and dizzy as I stood powerless to help her. A haze of smoke started to swirl around my head until I felt myself walking through a thick fog barely able to see my own hand in front of me. I knew from experience that I was walking through The Veil. The Veil is a place where trapped spirits lurk clinging onto every opportunity to cross over to our side. This is not a place for the living consciousness to linger. There are spirits here that have done unquestionable things that would turn even the hardest soul cold with fear. If you spend too much time in this place you too could lose your soul to the madness. Starting to panic, I could feel a sense of my body spinning, around and around my head started to spin. I closed my eyes trying to focus and trying to gain some sort of control. After what felt like minutes I opened my eyes and found myself in a small clearing in a forest, a couple of stone cottages in the background and to my right I could see a small crowd of people again dressed in a similar fashion to Margaret. They were gathered around a wooden stage. The staging was piled high with cuts of wood. Looking up I could see Margaret was tied to a large pole which had been erected in the centre of the wood pile.

I knew straight away what was going on. I was trying in my mind to wake up. As hard as I tried to bring myself out of the trance I was in, I was unable to wake up.

I could hear the sound of the men who were standing there shouting out the charges of witchcraft and of Margaret being in league with the devil.

I looked over at Margaret, her face bloody and bruised. It was obvious that she had been beaten and tortured, possibly being forced in to making a confession. As I stood watching and listening, Margaret looked straight over at me. With the entire trauma going around her, the shouting and screaming of the blood thirsty crowd I could sense a feeling of calm and acceptance in her eyes.

As one of the men lowered the burning torch to the wood pile, she smiled and nodded as if to alert me that she had accepted her fate. The shouting and chanting of the crowd was deafening; "witch, witch burn the witch".

I do not remember much from that point on, just being aware that I was back in the room with Margaret, the spirit standing before me. There were no words needed, just a sense that this vision was the final connection in our long journey together. To this day we have never spoken of the vison she gave me. I never asked what had happened, or what those men had done to her. I always felt that if I was supposed to know she would have told me.

This experience also gave me the rarely used but often useful ability to switch off and travel back in time with my psychic mind. There are several experiences of me traveling into The Veil and learning what lurks in there, which will be explained more later on.

Anyway, let's move on and start a new chapter with some cleansing experiences, starting with every little girl's best friend.

IS THAT GRANDAD ON THE WALL?

This is a very short story which I thought I would add in.

My mate Jack came round to stay one night. We would have been about 14 and we were watching horror movies in bed. I had my bedroom curtains open and the light of the moon had caused a silhouette of the window on the wall.

As we were watching the movie, we both noticed that a figure had also appeared on the wall as if someone was standing at the window. 'That looks like my granddad', I said 'wearing his long coat and cap'. 'Creepy', Jack replied. There was a knock on the door and mum poked her head in 'just letting you know your granddad has died'.

Jack and I looked at each other eyes open wide. We both looked over at the wall and the figure had disappeared.

Was this a coincidence or had Granddad come for a visit? I would like to think he did. What do you think?

MY DEAREST DEMON DOLLY

Dolls of all kinds have never been my favourite, especially the ones that people collect with real life faces and large curly hair; you know the ones from the 1990s that folk would buy and then have them standing in their living room cabinets. The dolls with their scary eyes which seem to follow you around the room. No matter where you stood, the creepy eyes would be still staring at you. On rare occasions, you would be sure that you even saw it move!

This case was my first experience with one of these dolls; it was part of an ongoing investigation that had led to the doll being used as a conduit for a demon.

I received a call from a lady from Glenrothes explaining to me that there had been a few strange things going in her home. As always, I was ready and eager to help! After arranging a time to go I went to pick up my friend Doreen who would come with me on some of my investigations.

On arriving at the address, we knocked on the door and were then greeted by a middle-aged lady who looked rather relieved that we had arrived.

We went straight into the front room where we could sit down, and I could do the necessary interview. This would give us an idea about what we were dealing with. There were a number of questions that needed to be asked to assess what the problem could be. Mrs X stated that around about a month ago she started to hear noises coming from the hallway. The noises were so loud that they were waking her up. I asked what time this was to which she replied around 3am. This is quite usual as it is this time that the veil between the living and dead is at its lowest. It is also the time that demons use as it mocks the trinity (the Father, the Son and the Holy Ghost).

Mrs X informed me that she had been feeling that something was watching her when she was in the kitchen. This feeling would follow her into the living room. Mrs X also stated that in the last week or so, the kitchen cupboards were opening and shutting on their own. Furthermore, she recounted that when she went into the kitchen a few days previously she had found the windows misted over with strange symbols written in the mist from the inside.

I was already reaching the conclusion that this may be a malevolent spirit. I asked her if there were any teenagers in the house to which she replied she had a 17-year-old son. I asked if there were any relationship problems, for example if she was arguing a lot with her partner. She answered that she was a single parent.

A teenager's hormones can attract spirit and, for unknown reasons, lots of arguing in the family can also be an indication of spirit in the house, or black magic being used.

Mrs X stated that on a few occasions she had woken up with small scratch marks on her legs and back. She explained that these felt hot and sore.

I asked if there had been any use of a Ouija board in the home, to which she replied 'no'. It was then time to have a walk about the property. I decided to use my dowsing rods to see if there was any unusual energy in the home. The rods were guiding me to go upstairs. I asked permission to go into every room which was granted. Doreen had decided to stay downstairs, as she was a little nervous. I went upstairs alone.

At the top of the stairs, I was drawn to the first bedroom to my right and as I entered, I felt a strong feeling that there was something not right in the room. 'Whose room is this?' I asked. Mrs X answered, 'my son's!'. Something bad had happened here and the residue of evil permeated my very soul. I was being drawn toward his bed. Apart from the stench of a sweaty teenager, there was the smell of sulphur which can be an indication of a demon.

Lifting the duvet, I peered under the bed. I would normally advise against looking under beds (especially if you have watched as many horror films as I have!). Anyway, looking under the bed I noticed that there was a large piece of cardboard. Grabbing it and pulling it out, I could see that it was a homemade Ouija board with a glass on top.

'Blooming heck!' I thought. Well, this explains a lot of things! There was also a bag of weed on the board. I took the board, glass and weed down to Mrs X. 'This will be the cause of all you goings on' I said as I handed her the items. 'The little bastard', replied Mrs X who was turning red with rage.

Looking behind Mrs X I could see Doreen looking rather disturbed and discreetly pointing her finger to the corner of the room. I looked towards where she was pointing and on the unit in the corner, I noticed one of those vile life-like dolls with blonde curly hair. As I looked closely, I could see that the doll was periodically blinking; its eyes slowly opening and shutting on their own....

'I think I have found where the demon is!'. Looking over to Mrs X the 'doll in the corner, where did it come from?'. 'It was a gift from my mother' Mrs X replied.

'I'm afraid the doll is being used as a conduit by the demon' I said. After bringing Margaret into the room, she was able to confirm my suspicions. I explained that my findings were that her son and one of his friends had been smoking weed while Mrs X was out working. While smoking the weed they were both playing on the Ouija board, which is probably one of the most dangerous things you can do when smoking weed, as weed lowers your senses meaning that spirits are able to take advantage of this and enter your personal space through the board.

In this case I believe that the demon had entered the doll and was then doing things around the house to torment Mrs X, causing her fear and anxiety. This fear and recognition would then feed the demon's energies making it even stronger.

The scratching of Mrs X's arms and back would be the demon trying to lower Mrs X's energies to the point that the demon would then be able to physically possess her; eventually take her soul.

I always recommend that if you do decide to do an Ouija board, always ensure that this is done with someone who is experienced, making sure that there is no alcohol or drug use. Remember to close the board down after you have finished.

'What happens now?' Mrs X asked. 'We take the doll out of the house, salt and burn the Ouija board, cleanse the house and ensure you make sure your son does not engage in this type of activity again', I replied.

I wrapped the doll up in a bag and placed it on the back seat of the car. I preceded to go back into the house to cleanse it with sage. I did ask Doreen to sit in the car and wait if she wanted to. Her reply was 'Not bloody likely!'.

After cleansing the house and leaving Mrs X with clear instructions on keeping her house safe, we drove back to my home, where I would then be able to deal with the possessed item. When dealing with possessed items, there are a number of important things to remember…

One thing you definitely should not do is either give the item away to or throw it away.

If you don't mind destroying the object, then the best way is to burn it (as fire has always been used in purification rituals). In this case, the doll was flammable so it could be burned. The best way to burn an object is to light your fire first, recite the Lord's Prayer or a similar prayer which you would be comfortable saying.

When the fire is going, place the object into the flames and command that the demon/spirit return hence to where it came from and to no longer torment the living. Watch and wait for the item to burn completely.

After the flames have died down, allow the ashes to cool down and pour salt into the ashes. Salt purifies spiritually. This spiritually purifying substance will ensure that the evil energy has completely left the remains. You can then gather up the ashes and place them in a bag or a jar.

You can take this jar or bag to a crossroads and bury it at the crossroads. Crossroads are sites where paths cross and over time many peoples' energies cross here also. It is believed that there is a link to the other side at a crossroads. Consequently, it is the best place to bury the remains of a possessed item. Margaret always says that you should never hang around a crossroads for too long as you can attract something unnatural and it can follow you home, so be warned!

If you can't burn the object then wrap it up in a cloth, say the Lord's Prayer, command that the demon/spirit return to hence where it came. You can place a religious icon in with the object should you wish to. It's always a good idea to collect these when you visit churches and temples, but please make sure they are not stolen; pay for them and ask for a blessing on the item. Having a few bottles of holy water is also useful as you can sprinkle holy water on the object as well. Take the item to a crossroads and dig deep hole. Place the object inside the hole and cover it with salt. Bury the item and walk away. Don't look back!

I can safely say that demon dolly dearest was burned and salted, placed in a jar, and now resides safely at a crossroads on the road between Kirkcaldy and East Wemyss.

As for Mrs X and her son, I do believe he was grounded for some time. Let's hope he learns his lesson and keeps away from the weed, and more importantly he does not play with Ouija boards. To this day Mrs X has not reported any further supernatural activity.

With regards getting rid of an evil spirit there are, as I have mentioned before, many rituals which one can perform. There is no right or wrong one; it is your intention that is important

coupled with your belief that you can move
that spirit on.

DEMON IN NICOL STREET FLATS

This next case is rather a bizarre one to which many of you may relate. Some of the experiences that are explained here may be experiences that you may have felt yourself, so be aware and brace yourself for this next story.

Have you ever woken up during the night and felt as if something was pressing down on your chest, you can open your eyes and see what's around you, but you feel as if you have been glued to the bed? Some call it night terrors and scientists have tried to explain that has something to do with the nervous system causing a form of temporary paralysis.

There are many written accounts of this in books from the occult and religious groups that explain that there are night demons or shadow demons that come into your room at night, normally around 3am (check the time the next time you experience it) and sit on your chest or their energy presses down on you. They do this to either possess you or to take your life force away from you.

It's interesting how Hollywood has latched on to this concept and have made dozens of movies involving night terrors in a paranormal way. I wouldn't say that everyone's experience with night terrors is paranormal, but it is interesting that a large percentage of people who experience this wake at 3am. It is believed that demons and evil spirits do this is in direct contradiction to the crucifixion of Christ.

My story starts at a time when I was living in Kirkcaldy in a complex of flats on Nicol Street. It was a nice flat with no negative feelings around it, pretty straight forward really with no causes for concern. While staying here we used to babysit my friends' two sons. One was 13 years old the other around 8 years old. This helped to give their mother a bit of a break.

The oldest son had a friend from school that happened to live in the flat bellow ours, and he would regularly go down and hang out with this friend while staying with us.

Now, I have to take you back a bit. I said previously that there was nothing negative about the flat and nothing had ever caused me concern from a paranormal perspective. However, approximately once a week I would wake up during the night with this hard pressing feeling on my chest. Yes, it was always around 3am, I would struggle to move but eventually would manage to move and free myself.

There was one night in particular when, yet again, I awoke with the pressing down feeling on my chest. As I opened my eyes, I was able to focus on a hooded figure that was hovering over the full length of my body. With my eyes now wide open, I focused on the hooded creature which was looking straight into my eyes; their green and red eyes staring down at me coupled with a piercing and menacing evil grin.

Again, I was in a situation where I was terrified. Instinctively, I started to scream while trying to focus on making this thing go away! The pressing feeling was getting firmer and firmer. 'Where the hell is Margaret or even bloody Albert?'. With all my effort and might I managed to get rid of the creature floating above me. I started to have these same experiences on a weekly basis, usually on a Thursday. It was becoming rather tiresome.

Let's get back on track! On this occasion when we were babysitting, the oldest lad asked if he could go down and play some games on the X-box with their friend after tea. As always, I agreed saying 'be back by 9'. Around 10 minutes after he had left, the door opened; he was back with a rather concerned look on his face.

'What's happened?', I asked. 'I can't play with Charlie tonight as his parents are having friends over tonight for their session on the Ouija board'! I was flabbergasted and replied 'bloomin' heck! I wouldn't have guessed that they were into all of that kind of stuff'. That night we decided to have a DVD and chill out night.

After going to bed, I woke with a fright during the night., 'What the hell is going on?', I started to think, as the pressing started again on my chest. Opening my eyes, yet again the hooded creature was floating above me. This time I could feel a tight grip around my throat. It was getting tighter and tighter. I was struggling to breathe as the grip intensified. With my left I reached, over to my bedside post where I keep several items, hanging just in case! I managed to grab a rosary that one of the Nuns from the Dysart Carmel monastery had gifted to me. Holding it in my hand and facing it towards the creature, I started to demand that it release me and leave. I demanded it to leave for a second time. This time its grip became lighter. I commanded it to leave a further time and with that it released me and left.

I lay there on my back drained of all energy, fearful and stressed. Looking over at the clock, it was 3am (of course).

Now this continued for the period of time I lived in that flat. Several months after the ordeal described. we decided to sell the flat and move. I am thankful to say that the creature never appeared to me in the new home. However recently these night terrors have again started, is it connected to the house I currently live? Well, that's a different story.

BURN BETTY BURN

Working in the psychic and cleansing industry I often get called to investigate lots of different disturbances, strange activities, objects moving or disappearing or just generally something not being right.

The next few chapters are a collection of some of my investigations in and around the Fife area.

Please note that people's names and places are changed to protect the identity of those involved.

The first case involves a call I received from a family living in a coastal village in East Fife. The family lived in a semi-detached house.

Upon arriving I ask the usual questions: Is anyone in the house taking drugs? Are there teenagers? Is there un-happiness within the relationship? And so on. This gives me an indication if the problem is physical or paranormal.

The couple I visited were both in their mid-30s. They were your average working couple probably ready to start having a family and settling down.

After arriving and introducing myself I sat down in their living room and asked what had been going on to cause them to seek help.

In my experience it is often the women that are more open-minded about these things, but in this case the husband was the one who was more eager to get the situation sorted.

'We moved here about a year ago and things were great in the first two or three weeks, and then we started to notice that things were going missing. First it was my watch, then my wife's gran's ring disappeared. A shoe or item of clothing would then disappear. These items would turn up again but in a place that we both know we wouldn't have put them.'

'My wife started to get scared when she was in the house on her own, feeling that something was watching her.'

'Yes', she replied, 'I was in the kitchen pottering about, and I suddenly felt as if someone had walked in and was standing behind me. I have watched loads of horror films and it didn't give me that chilled and cold feeling, it was totally the opposite I felt a hot burning sensation all over my body.'

'That's not the first time either', the husband continued. 'It can be a cold day, or the central heating is turned off and in certain areas of the house you can feel really hot spots as if there is a heat lamp shining above you. I admit it all sounds very bizarre but what made us call you was that me and my wife were putting some clothes back in the wardrobe and I noticed a burning smell inside the wardrobe. We moved a couple of shirts that were hanging up and noticed that several of them had been badly singed. Even some of my wife's clothes were burnt as well. How the hell does that happen without a fire?'

'Ok' I replied. 'Has anything else been happening that is out of the ordinary?', I asked.

'At night when we go to bed, my wife and I get the sensation or feeling that there is something in the room with us. We can even hear a faint screaming. We thought at first that it was cats fighting outside, but it continued every night. It was only faint but, it was definitely a screaming in agony; a painful scream.'

After listening to the couple and drinking several cups of coffee, I concluded that there was something paranormal going on in the couple's house.

It is at this point that I normally ask if I can have a walk around each room on my own and try to tune into any spirits or entities that may be lurking.

I started to go into each of the rooms. There was very little I could pick up apart from the spirit of an infant. 'Have you lost a child?', I asked. 'I had a miscarriage a couple of years ago', the wife replied.

I did not feel that this infant was the cause of the problems so I continued with my investigation. When entering the bedroom, I could feel that something didn't feel right, but even when focusing my mind, I could not feel any spirits directly in the room. I took out my spirit dowsing rods to see if there was any energy in the room and to see in which direction any potential energy was coming from.

Dowsing rods are mainly used for finding water, but if used correctly can also point you in the direction of spirit energy.

Using the dowsing rods, I was able to detect that the spiritual energy was coming from the wall where the wardrobe was standing. 'What's behind this wall I asked?'. 'Our next-door neighbour's house' the wife replied. I realised then that the spirit was coming through the wall into the couple's room. Further investigation was going to be required.

'Do you know if there have been any strange deaths in the homes around you?' I asked. 'Not really. We basically keep ourselves to ourselves'. I guess that some further leg work would be required, to try to determine who the spirit was, and what they wanted.

You should remember that you can't just knock on someone's door and say, 'Hello, I'm investigating a paranormal haunting in the home next door. Has anyone died in your house?'.

I put my coat on and went to the next-door neighbour's home, knocked on the door and eagerly waited. The door opened and a middle-aged man answered. After introducing myself, I asked him the said, 'I'm writing a ghost story book and am currently doing a little research. Has there been any strange happenings or occurrences that you would like me to add to my book?'. 'F^&& off you weirdo!' was the response as he slammed the door in my face.

'Well, this is going great', I thought. I managed to chat to several of the residents in the road, but none had any tales to tell. One lady told me that some of the local cats had gone missing, but nothing to give me an indication of anything paranormal. There was still a couple of houses to do, but I wasn't holding out much hope for any answers. Walking up the pathway of the next house, I noticed how nice the garden was; it looked extremely well kept with lots of older flowers and plants you don't often see.

As I was approaching the door, I could see the curtains twitching. I knocked and waited. After a minute or so, an elderly lady opened the door and with a rather friendly and kind face said, 'Yes me dear, how can I help?'. 'Hi. Thank you for coming to the door. I am asking around the neighbours if they could help me with a project. I'm investigating a haunting of a particular house and I was wondering if you know of anything in the past that has happened here that may cause a haunting?'. For some unknown reason I felt I had to tell this woman the real reason for my visit.

The old lady looked puzzled at first and then looked up at me saying, 'well, the only thing I could think of was poor wee Betty McBain; the little girl who died in the house over the road'.

'Are you able to tell be about it?', I asked her.

'I think it would have been about 1947. I was a young girl at the time and Betty was in the older girls' class at the school I went to, so she would have been around 10 years old. As far as I can recall, it was one evening around Christmas time. Yes, I recall! It had been snowing. I think the fire started at night. It was a Tilley lamp that had fallen and smashed'.

'The fire took hold very quickly, engulfing the house and spreading fast. I remember the noise of the fire engine coming up the street. I was watching from my bedroom window. Look up, it's the window above us.'

She continued to tell me, 'I saw Betty's parents and her wee brother Billy standing on the street. They couldn't get to Betty because of the smoke'.

'I looked and could see her in the window screaming; flames coming up around her. The firemen did break the window to try and get her out, but it was too late. I think the fire and smoke had taken her.'

'It must have been awful', I said looking over the road to the house.

'Ooh it was!" she said. 'Her parents never got over it. Even when the house was repaired her parents wouldn't move back to the house. I heard they moved to start a new life. Betty is buried at the Kirk in the village; a small grave all forgotten, I guess. Do you know what son, I think I will take a walk down there and put some flowers down.' She looked at me I could tell that it had saddened her to recall the story.

"Thank you for telling me what had happened, it has helped me a lot and I know what I can do to help the couple in the house.'

After thanking her again, I went back to where the couple lived. After knocking on the door and being invited back in, I sat down and explained to the couple what my investigation had come up with.

I relayed the story of what had happen to little Betty McBain and that I believed that it was her spirit that was trapped in the time of her death. She may be replaying her death. This was the energy which was coming into the couple's house. I also believed that the couple may have reminded Betty of her own parents and that is why she had latched onto them.

'Oh my God', the wife said. 'That's horrible! What the hell do we do? I can't stay here if that is what's going to continue to happen.'

'Try not to panic!' I replied. 'I don't think Betty is going to hurt you in any way. She is simply trapped here and needs to move on'. I felt the best thing we could was to start with was a house cleansing and blessing. I went back to the car and gathered the items, a Rosary, sage, and salt water.

Going to the bedroom I called upon Margaret and the spirits and workers of the light to help Betty to move forward and over to the other side. Burning the sage and focusing to see beyond the veil I called out to Betty. "I'm calling you Betty McBain please come forward and do not be afraid, we are here to help you, Betty please come forward."

I could feel that Betty was resisting me and was reluctant to come forward. I turned to Margaret and asked to check to see if Betty's parents were on the other side. A couple of minutes later Margaret reappeared 'Her mother and father are there but her brother Billy is still alive and is currently in Stratheden' (The local mental health Hospital). Could Billy have been the cause of the fire?

'Betty! Margaret and I are here to help you, your mum and dad are waiting for you' I could hear a faint voice to my left-hand side as the room became warmer, 'They don't love me or want me! They only wanted to save Billy'.

'Hello Betty', I replied. 'Your Mummy and Daddy do love you. The fire was so bad they could not reach you and by the time help came it was too late'. 'Why did they leave?', she asked. 'Sometimes things and memories are too hard to live with and I believe your parents moved away because they could not deal with the pain of losing you".

I felt that we were getting through to her so I upped the game 'Margaret here can take you to your parents and you will then see them again, they are waiting for you just follow Margaret into the light.'

'Do you promise?', she asked. 'Absolutely', I replied, and with that I felt a cool breeze and the spirit of Betty McBain had crossed over. There was a feeling of lightness and calm back in the room.

I turned to the couple and told them that Betty had crossed over and she was at peace. 'Thank you so much', the husband said 'is there anything we need to do?', he asked.

'I just need to salt and bless the room and bless the rest of the house, to make sure there is no more residual energy in the house.' This did not take long and with that I wished he couple well and said my goodbyes. I did inform them not to encourage any spiritual activity in the house and to call me in a couple of weeks' time to let me know that they were ok.

Driving out of the street I decided to stop at the local shops and buy a small bunch of flowers, I then drove to the village Kirk, getting out of my car I walked into the small cemetery, looking around each of the graves it took me around 20 minutes to find the small simple headstone of Betty McBain covered in moss and overgrown, very much forgotten.

Margaret appeared at my side, 'good job you did there, sunshine', she said 'she is now in the light of her parents love and is now finally at rest, but there is something I am a bit confused with" she said, 'it wasn't a lamp that started the fire!'.

Albert then appeared in front of me. 'Be careful Joe. There are dark forces at play here and they are not happy with what you have just done'. As always, he then disappeared without any more explanation.

Spending round 30 minutes cleaning and tidying the grave I lay the flowers down, standing up I took a couple of minutes to ponder on the experience I had with wee Betty McBain.

'Rest in peace Betty. Gone but not forgotten".

THE WRITING'S ON THE WALL

This next case is one of those cases which still baffles and leads me to question why someone would want to bring evil into their homes.

It was a short time after the case of Betty McBain that I received a call from a John Tyler and Kate Tyler. On the initial call they had informed me that they were experiencing a few issues in their home. They told me that their four-year-old daughter was having nightmares often waking up in the night screaming. Both John and Kate had experienced a strange feeling in the bedroom. Kate reported she was waking up in the night with the feelings of something pressing on her chest whilst being unable either to move or to scream.

As always, I arranged a time to give them a house call. I packed a few items in a bag; sage, dowsing rods, a rosary, salt and a crucifix.

On arriving at the address, I walked up the pathway. Looking up at the bedroom window I could see the faint figure of a hooded entity. It appeared to be gazing down at me.

I knocked loudly on the door; if there was something in the house, I wanted it to know that I meant business and I was not afraid. The door opened and John was at the door with his daughter behind him. 'Hello Joe. Thanks for coming. This is Polly-Ann' he said, looking down at his daughter. 'Come in come in' he beckoned as he opened the door wider. I walked in and Kate, his wife, was standing in the hallway. 'Hi' she said in a friendly relieved tone.

It was at this point that I felt a sharp pain in the back of my left calf muscle. No, it wasn't supernatural; it was Polly-Ann kicking me.

'Ouch please don't kick me', I said turning around and giving her a bit of a scowl. 'Sorry about that. Polly-Ann! No! Please don't kick our visitors!', her father said looking rather embarrassed.

'Coffee would be good' I said as I entered the front room. Sitting down on the sofa I asked Kate what had been happening, whilst her husband made the coffee.

'It started about six months ago', Kate began. 'We had a bit of a Tarot party with a few friends around. It all went really well, a bit of a laugh and a drink. You know, nothing to serious.'. I asked Kate if people were drinking before getting their readings and whether the tarot reader was ok with this. She answered that yes, people had been drinking and this didn't seem to bother the reader.

I asked her to tell me what had been happening since that night.

'It really started to happen that night. Everyone had gone and John and I had checked in on Polly-Ann. She was fast asleep. We went into the kitchen to tidy up and put the dishwasher on. It was then that we heard Polly-Ann screaming'.

John came into the room and handed me my coffee. It was at this moment that Polly Ann decided to give me another kick. 'Please continue' I said giving the perpetrator another scowl.

'We both went into Polly-Ann's room. She was sitting up in bed crying, saying that the scary man was in the corner of her room. I looked and there was nothing there. I put it down to the fact she was having a bad dream".

John started to speak 'a couple of days later, we were watching tv and the channel changed on its own. The remote was on the coffee table. I thought it was the battery running low, so I changed it. Within an hour the channel changed again. It was bit freaky, but we thought it was just a fault; it happened a couple of times'.

'About a week, later the lights started to flicker, and we could hear a faint knocking. Knock.

Knock. Knock. Repeated every now and then', Kate continued.

Again, Polly-Ann started to annoy me by kicking me. Her mother continued, 'Yes Polly-Ann started to play up as well, becoming stubborn and naughty. She is normally such a good girl".

'The knocking three times is generally an indication of an evil presence', I explained. 'Have there been any other incidences", I asked, looking up at Kate and John. It was at this point that I noticed the outline of a partly transparent figure standing in the corner of the room. I did not want to say anything at this point as I did not want to alarm the couple who remained oblivious to this presence.

'Yes', said Kate, 'I have had a couple of occasions where I have woken up in the night and have felt a pressure pushing down upon me. I try to scream, but I can't. I can't even move; it's awful'.

'Has this been at around 3am?' I asked. 'Yes, 3 am every time', she replied. 'How did you know?'.

'Let's continue with the investigations!', I replied. This time I noticed the figure had moved upstairs to where Polly-Ann was sitting playing. 'Yes', John replied.

John continued, 'Polly-Ann was coming down the stairs and I was at the bottom watching her take her time. I heard a growl and Polly-Ann started to fall. It wasn't like a normal fall; it was as if she had been pushed'. To be honest, after having been kicked repeatedly, I could not help but empathise with something which might want to push her down the stairs! I had to stop myself from thinking such wicked thoughts!

Avoiding the temptation to praise the actions of this entity I simply replied with 'That's not very good. Does Polly-Ann have lots of nights where she wakes crying?'. 'Yes', said Kate 'it's always the same; she cries saying the scary man woke her up. She has been sleeping in our room a lot. I am starting to feel drained and tired all the time. I have even had to be signed off work."

I looked over to Polly-Ann and this time the figure had moved over towards the kitchen door. I tried not to let on that I could see the entity. If it had clocked on that I could see it, it may have been dangerous for the family or even me. Something evil was in this house and I felt that this family were in grave danger.

I asked the couple if there was anyone who could look after Polly-Ann for a couple of days while we tried to sort this problem out.

'John's mum just lives down the road. We could ask her', Kate replied. 'That's a good idea" I said. 'Do you want to call her and see if you can drop her off today?', I asked. 'Yes, I will do it right away', she responded.

Coming back into the room after a short call, she said that it was fine, and John would be able to take her round.

Kate went up to Polly-Ann's room to pack a few things. Moments after going upstairs, Kate started to shout, 'come upstairs! Come upstairs!'.

I looked at John and told him to stay with Polly-Ann while I went to see what the problem was. 'I'm in here', Kate said as she called me into Polly-Ann's room. 'Can you smell that?', she asked. It was the smell of sulphur, like the smell of rotting eggs.

'Please hurry and pack some things!', I said. 'Whatever is in your house is aware of what is going on, so time is now of the essence'.

I did not need Margaret, dowsing rods or to look into the veil to know that there was something wrong. With a few things packed and putting Polly-Ann's coat on, John left to take her to his mother's.

'While John is gone, I will have a look around the house to see what we are dealing with' I informed Kate. I took out my crucifix and rosary, got myself into the zone and started to walk through each room of the house. As I walked into the dining room, Margaret appeared. 'There are four entities in this house', she said, 'be careful!'. 'I'm on it!' I replied.

Looking in the dining room, I was drawn to the far left hand corner where I could see the outline of what looked half man half goat. It had yellow eyes which were gazing at me. Holding my crucifix in my right hand and grasping my rosary in the left, I closed my eyes. 'Be gone evil one!' I commanded.

I heard a hiss as I repeated 'In the name of God I command you to be gone.' I felt that this had caused the entity to go.

Coming out of the dining room I turned and went up the stairs. With each step I could feel a heavy feeling pressing down upon my shoulders; pressing harder and harder with each step I made. Entering Polly- Ann's room again, I could see the outline of a man in the room. This I felt, was a human spirit. I summoned Margaret. 'Leave this one with me!' she said. 'I will deal with him'.

I entered the couple's bedroom. Floating above the bed I could see another entity. It was dark in appearance and again had those yellow menacing eyes.

'I am not afraid of you', I said in a strong deep voice. Even though I was shitting myself inside! 'What is it you want?', I asked in a direct tone. 'Death is what I want, little man', It replied. I was becoming quite anxious and was wondering how I was going to be able to deal with this.

As I wanted to see where the fourth entity had gone, I made my way back down the stairs. I had last seen this entity as it was heading into the kitchen. Walking into the kitchen, I could see that it was probably the original one that had been put in when the house was built. There against the wall, I could see the entity I was looking for. This was the entity I had seen when I first entered the house. It was standing in the kitchen by the wall units.

It looked me in the eyes. I could hear what sounded like laughing. 'You think you can get rid of us?', it jeered. Its voice rang in my head. 'You are nothing, just an insect ready to be crushed it cursed' it mocked.

I turned away so that my thoughts and energy would not feed it. It was at this point that I heard the front door; it was John returning.

I went back into the front room and asked the couple to sit down while I told them what I had found.

'You have four entities in this house, one human spirit and 3 demonic or evil spirits. Somehow the 3 evils spirits have been able to enter your home. The human spirit was probably here before and was trapped. My spirit companion has managed to move that spirit over to the other side, but the other three are stronger and will not go so readily'.

'What do we do?', John asked. 'You have to trust me and do exactly what I say', I commanded. 'How did they get here?', Kate asked.

I began to explain by saying, 'I think the energy build-up of the tarot party has somehow opened a doorway or given off a beacon, I am unsure at this time. There is a goat like entity in the dining room. This is a minor demonic entity, mischievous in its actions, but not harmful. It should, however, not be here.'

'The one in your bedroom is what I term a 'Shadow Demon'. These are creatures that destroy and drain you. They are incredibly dangerous, especially when you are feeling vulnerable.'

'It is the third entity that worries me the most. This is a parasitic demon, feeding off your fear, especially off Polly-Ann as she is very spirited. This is what it is drawn to. It will eventually kill you. Some evil spirits are drawn to the life energy of children. That is why it is draining the both of you. You both need to be strong; together we can win this battle.'

As we sat on the sofa, I could see that my explanation of what I had found had profoundly shocked the couple. Well, wouldn't you be a little shocked after hearing that kind of news?

'So, what do we do now?', Kate asked. 'Do we move house?'

'The first thing we need to do is to do a total house cleansing. We need to try to move the entities out of the house and back to where they have come from', I explained.

'I will need you to do exactly what I say and not to show any fear at all. Firstly, we need to open some windows and cover any mirrors which you may have in the house.'

Opening the windows encourages cleansing in the house and I believe that spirits and entities can hide in the reflections of mirrors.

I took out my rosary and sage smudging stick asking the husband to walk around me and repeat the words I say when performing the cleansing. 'We shall start in dining room. I need both of you to be strong. The entity may try to scare you or communicate with you. The entity will tell you lies. Do you understand? If it gets too bad, close your eyes, and think positive thoughts'.

Going into the dining room the entity was there again lurking in the shadows. 'They do this. Lurking in the shadows is what the love, drawing from your energies like a parasite.' I stared the entity in the eyes, took a deep breath and said a small prayer in my head. I lit the sage stick and circling the smoke clockwise I commanded the following:

'I call upon the workers and spirits of light to come and surround this house and room with light and love. With the powers of three times three, I command this evil to leave'.

The entity looked me up and down and laughed. 'You think your petty witchcraft can get rid of me? I will tear this family apart. There is nothing you can do to harm me!'.

Again, I took a deep breath. 'Evil spirit worker of the darkness you are not welcome here. In the name of all that is good I command you to leave'.

Still circling the sage smoke, I directed the smoke to where the entity was standing. Margaret appeared beside me and started to chant 'by the power of mother earth I command you to leave'. I looked to John and told him to repeat after me 'You are not welcome here. I have power over you. This is my home. Leave now and be gone forever'.

John nervously repeated this with his wife Kate joining in. I was impressed how strong they were being. It was almost as if they were getting into it big time!

Looking at the weakened spirit, I commanded it again to leave. With the combined energies of Margaret, Kate and John and me, the entity weakened, disappeared through the wall, and was gone. I turned to the couple 'that's one down! Let's go upstairs and sort out that Shadow Demon!'.

As we went up the stairs, I could sense that the Shadow Demon knew it was next on our list. It was bracing itself for a fight.

I walked into the bedroom and immediately felt a burning sting on my right cheek. 'Ouch', I yelped. 'Bloody hell', John shouted. 'It's just bloody scratched him!'. 'I'm ok', I replied.

As the three of us entered the room, the Shadow Demon was floating above our heads around 2 feet in front of us. 'Oh my God!" Kate screamed. 'I have scratch marks on my arm'.

'Don't panic!' I shouted, 'This is what it wants; it wants to scare you'. 'Well, it's doing a bloody good job!', John shouted. 'It's getting physical; I don't like it!".

I gave my crucifix to Kate and asked her to keep repeating 'In the name of Jesus Christ, I command you to leave'. 'Just hold it up in front of you and keep repeating the phrase. Do not stop until I say, and do not open your eyes', I instructed. 'John, you need to command it to leave your home. This is your home and you and Kate will not let it hurt your family'.

With Margaret at my side, I felt like we were the cast of The A-Team. Margaret started waving her finger in the air drawing symbols and chanting her incantations to remove the spirit.

Looking directly at the shadow demon, I started to wave the smudge stick, commanding the shadow demon to leave. 'Be gone evil one. You are not welcome here. Be gone! The workers of light command you to be gone. The spirits of old command you to be gone. I command you to be gone. You have no power here'.

This I repeated and repeated. God knows what the neighbours would have felt if they could hear what was going on! I did not care; we had a job to do. After around 10 minutes the shadow demon started to scream at me about what it was going to do to me; 'I'm going to tear your head off. I am going to kill your mother. I will kill your family. I will burn you up and drag you down with me'.

As I continued chanting, a burning sensation started on my chest, neck and back. I could feel the scratches penetrating my skin.

With Margaret moving closer and closer, I felt the shadow demon was losing its grip. With a nice and sharp bite on my arm it finally disappeared.

'Christ!' said John, 'you're covered in scratches and bites!'.

'It's ok', I replied 'we just need to rest for a while. Let's go into the dining room.'

'What do we do now?', Kate asked. 'Well, I don't know about you, but I think I am going to order a Chinese takeaway!'.

I must admit the look on their faces was a picture. Anyway, they decided it was a good idea and so we ordered some food. It was a well-deserved break. It's always good to recharge before tackling more entities. I had a feeling that the demon in the kitchen may be hard work.

'Well, I think it's time we finished what we started', I said as I devoured the last part of my meal. I picked up the sage and crucifix and made my way into the kitchen. As we walked into the kitchen, I had a feeling that the evil entity was geared up and ready for us. I could see it in the corner by one of the units. It was hissing and spitting foul obscenities at me. As I started to smoke the room it said, 'I will tear out your tongue'. It shouted at me and threatened to pull out both of my eyes and then to stab me in the heart with its claw.

'I command you to leave this house' I shouted as I continued to wave the sage stick in the air. 'This is a home of love and peace. Your presence is not welcome here. You must leave'.

The evil entity scowled and hissed as I started to move forward. Again, I could feel the entity bite my arms and legs as it fought back.

By now, I was becoming increasingly tired as the night went on. It felt as if all of the chanting, cleansing and the sage were no longer making any difference to the entity. It all seemed futile.

Margaret appeared again. 'This entity is really strong. It's from the old stock from millennia ago, maybe before humans were on the earth. Something strong has brought it through.'

I was unsure if I could get rid of this entity and started to doubt myself.

It was at this point that Albert appeared. 'Call the entity forward and I will drag it down below'. Closing my eyes, I commanded the entity to appear. As it came out from one of the units on the wall, I could see Albert reach out. Wrapping his arms around the entity's twisted neck, he started to drag the entity down through the floor. Just as it was going down it managed to get one last swipe across my leg. It gave me a scar I still carry to this day.

I turned to Margaret and looked at her. She could see what I was thinking. 'Is Albert a Demon?' I asked. She looked at me and said, 'Yes he is, but don't let that affect you. He is on the fence as they say' (now, that's another story).

'I think there is something behind the unit' Margaret said pointing to from where the entity had appeared. I turned to a stunned John and Kate. 'We need to see what is behind the unit. Can you remove it for us to have a look?'.

John went to fetch his toolbox while Kate emptied the unit of its contents. After several minutes of unscrewing, the unit was off the wall. Behind the unit was a wall decorated with ugly 60s wallpaper.

'What now?' John asked. 'We need to scrape off the wallpaper and see what's there', I replied. 'I have a strong feeling that something is not right'. 'I think I have some scrappers in the shed', John said. 'I will get them. Kate, can you dampen the wall while I fetch them, please?'.

After dampening the wall John came in with two scrapers. We began to scrap the paper off the wall. As we were peeling the paper off, I started to notice black shapes and writing on the wall. The more paper we removed, the more shapes and writing was unveiled. Once all the wallpaper had been removed I could clearly see that there were some sort of satanic symbols and verse on the wall.

'I have a feeling that this is how the entities were getting through. I think we will need to remove them with salt water and then bless the whole house', I said.

Kate filled the basin with hot water and added the salt to the water. I lit the sage and blessed the water and then with some sponges we started to clean the markings off the wall. After about 30 minutes they had gone.

'It is time to bless and cleanse the house and to make sure that nothing comes back again', I said. I went from room to room calling the four corners and asking for light and good to be in the house.

After this was done, I informed John and Kate that they had to ensure that they did not do anything that would bring the entities back into the house; to avoid anything to do with spirits and the occult. All that was left for them to do was to settle back and relax, and wait for the return of their own little demon Polly-Ann.

DON'T LOSE YOUR HEAD, ESPECIALLY IN A HOT TUB.

Many moons ago while living in Fife, I used to do regular Tarot parties, where around 10 people would gather, and each would have a reading in turn. There were strict rules that they would have to follow, no recording, no drugs, no joking around and definitely no drinking before their reading.

This next case may seem a little far-fetched to some but believe me it is a case that to this day remains one of my most evidential and strong cases that spirits are real and that they can help you and warn you of impending danger.

It started with the booking of a tarot party around 30 miles from where I was living in

Kirkcaldy. I had to go to a small town in the area of Perth and Kinross. I had been booked by a nurse called Janet. During the initial conversation, I had explained the rules which needed to be followed.

On the date arranged, I gathered my equipment (candles, cards, and sage). Driving to Janet's seemed a long journey. It was 5pm and I had already done a full day's work, so I was tired. As I drove along the dual carriageway, I felt a cold sensation running down my spine. I looked into my wing mirror. Looking back at me was the spirit of a young woman in her early to mid-twenties. Her face was all cut and bruised. On her left temple I could see a split in her head with what appeared to be blood and brain seeping out. It's certainly something that you don't really want to see while driving on your own on a busy carriageway. This sort of occurrence happens a lot and is more common than people probably realise. The next time you are alone in the car driving home at night, just check your wing mirror now and then, if you dare! You may just catch a glimpse.

'I died over there', the woman said. 'I fell off the back of Dave's bike. I told him he was going too fast, but he would not slow down. The bike shuddered and I came off. I smashed my head open, so I did. Dave just drove off and left me. It took me 8 hours to die. I wait here waiting for Dave to come back, but he never does'.

I looked in the mirror again to say how sorry I was, but she had disappeared. She was obviously trapped in that area unable to move on. This can happen when spirits are yanked out of their bodies and then the person is unable to move on; sometimes living the event over and over again.

Janet lived in a lovely town house with a gorgeous, sheltered back garden, a nice hot tub and garden furniture. There were already some guests at the home, all getting ready to have their reading. I introduced myself and asked which room I was going to be reading in. Janet replied that it was going to be done in her bedroom.

I asked her if everyone had complied to the previously agreed rules of the reading. She confirmed they had. I made my way in the room and set my cards out. I lit the sage and cleansed the room; I do this to ensure that no negative energies are in the room.

I was ready for my first victim! I felt that the night had gone very well. Each person having a reading was very pleasant and open-minded which makes the job of the reader so much easier. As the night was drawing to an end, Janet was the last of the guests to have her reading.

With her sitting down in front of me, I started to focus the images I need to see to conduct the reading. I could see that she had been married and this marriage had ended in divorce, with her husband leaving her for someone else. This she confirmed. I also saw the image of a nurse, which she confirmed was her job. I received the name Pete which she confirmed was her new partner, whom she had just started seeing. I then explained that I could smell gas. She informed me that Pete was a gas engineer.

I felt the reading was going really well with lots of information and messages coming through. It was then that I looked up at her. Behind her I could see the spirit of a lady who gave me the name Fran.

'Who is Fran?', I asked 'that's my mum' Janet replied, covering her mouth in shock. 'Is she here?' she asked. 'Yes" I replied, 'she wants to say thank you for putting her favourite bracelet into the coffin. She was very grateful as it meant so much to her.'

'Oh my God! That's the bracelet I brought her with my pocket money when I was little; she never took it off!'

I was pleased that I was bringing some comfort to Janet. I was able to tell her that mother was ok, that she was very proud of what she had achieved, and that she popped in to see her now and then.

It was then that I felt a faint feeling come over me. I developed a light-headed feeling which made me sit back into the chair. Closing my eyes, I tried to refocus. Was it the readings that I had done had worn me out, or was something wrong?

I opened my eyes again and I could see that I was back in the room where Janet was lying on her bed. The door opened and a man in a balaclava walked in holding a large kitchen knife. He walked over to where Janet was lying and stabbed her in the chest several times. I could hear her screaming as the knife ripped through her chest. Three more stabs and she was dead. The masked man slit her throat for good measure.

I believe this vision was causing me to scream as at that moment I could feel myself being shaken by Janet. 'What's wrong? What's wrong?', she shrieked. I opened my eyes and looked straight at her. 'I'm so sorry, I just had an awful vision' I replied.

'For Christ's sake, you freaked me out!' she replied. 'What did you see? You need to tell me!' she asked. I looked at her again. 'I'm not sure I can', I replied. 'I want to know if it is something bad', she said. 'Yes' was my simple reply. I was unsure if I should tell her, but she persisted. I looked over at her bed where her mother was now standing. The spirit of her mother said, 'You need to tell her. Please, please! Tell my baby what you saw'.

'Are you sure you want to know what I saw?' I asked, just to confirm that Janet really wanted to hear what I was going to say. 'Please tell me. I need to know!'', she implored.

I told her what I had seen. I told her that her life was in danger, that I had seen her murder and that she was going to stabbed to death and have her throat cut. I explained that I felt the vison was a warning for her to leave her house; her life was in danger if she stayed.

She looked shocked and shaken but agreed that I was right to tell her.

Some who work in this field of the paranormal believe that we should never tell people the bad things we see. My answer to that would be that if you were given the vision, or the message then that person has the right to know, even if it is something bad and evil. I know that I would want to know. It is for this reason that I always explain to the person that I will tell them the whole message (both good and bad) when doing a reading. I believe that this empowers the person who can then decide whether to continue to have the reading, or not.

Anyway, let's get back to the case! I apologised for having to give her the message but explained that I felt that her mother was giving her the warning, (as some believe that spirits know the future).

As Janet's was the last reading of the evening, I cleansed the room and packed up my things. I could tell that Janet was a bit shaken, so asked one of her friends if she could keep an eye on her as she had had a bit of a shock.

I bid my farewells and left. Getting into my car I looked back at the house. I could not help but think that this was not going to end well.

The next day I went into work as normal. My reception staff were in before me and had prepared my rota for the day. A full day of patients and readings was ahead of me, even though I was still tired from the night before. I would simply have to press on.

It was around lunch time when my receptionist knocked on the door. 'There is a Janet on the phone. She wants to speak to you', she said. 'Ok put her through', I replied. 'Here we go!' I thought; she is going to have a right go at me about the reading she had had.

"Hi this is Janet. I just wanted to let you know that I couldn't stay in the house last night; I was scared out of my wits!'.

I tried to reiterate that I am not able to dictate what the spirits decide to tell you, and that her mother was trying to give her a warning. I advised her that the best thing, she could do was either to heed the warning, or take her chances that the spirits were wrong. In clear frustration, Janet put the phone down.

Around about five months later my receptionist came into my office to let me know that a Janet was on the phone asking to talk to me. It had been such a long-time since her reading that I had forgotten who she was, and what she might be calling for.

I picked up the phone. 'Hello. How can I help?', I asked. 'Hi', she said. 'I don't think you will remember me, but you came to my house some months ago to do a Tarot party. When I had my reading, you told me that my mother was with us and that she had a message for me. You told me that my life was in danger and that my mother had said that I was going to get my throat slit in my bed'.

'Oh yes', I replied, 'I remember you. I'm glad that you are ok and well'.

'I'm just phoning to thank you as you have saved my life.', she replied. 'After the reading, I couldn't stay in the house; I was too frightened. I went to stay with a friend. After a couple of weeks my friend asked if I wanted to move in permanently. I decided that I could rent my house out'.

I listened intently as she continued.

'If you look in the local paper today, you will see that there was a double murder in my house. I still can't believe it, but drug dealers had got the wrong house. They broke into my house and killed the boyfriend, who was in the hot tub, with an axe. They then went upstairs into my bedroom and slit the girlfriend's throat whilst she was lying in bed. I just can't believe this has happened. I wanted to call you to thank you for saving my life'.

I was very touched that she felt the need to do this; I was only passing on the message from her mother. 'Thank you, Janet, for letting me know that you're ok. It is your mother who is to thank; it is amazing that although she is dead, she is still looking after you', I said. With that we said our good-byes.

It is my strong belief that spirit will always look out for us and help us when they can.

Even though Janet was saved by the message from her mother, there was still a double murder. Unfortunately, a couple lost their lives in the process. I will always remember them and spare a thought for their spirits in the hope that they have found rest and peace.

It was shortly after this event that I decided to stop doing Tarot parties; they drain me of too much energy.

It is always good to note that if you do have a reading of any kind, it takes a lot of energy from the spirit to come through. As Margret once told me 'it's like trying to push your fat arse through the eye of a needle'.

So please take note, especially if the spirits have come forward to give you a warning, or to give you some good advice.

There have been so many times that Margaret has brought through family members for the person having the reading and with the spirit's advice being to leave a job or a negative situation. Too often the person having the reading chooses not to act on the advice. This makes spirit mad and frustrated, especially if the situation is harming the person getting the reading. All the spirits want to do is to see them happy; listen to their advice!

WARNING IN THE TAPE THAT COULD NOT BE HEARD

I often get asked if people can record their readings and my answer will always be 'no'!

Some find this very hard to understand and can get very frustrated, as some Tarot readers allow this.

I did allow this in the past, but this next story convinced me that for me, it was not the best idea.

I know that there are many people who do not like the sound of their own voice when it is recorded and being played back to them. Personally, I hate the sound of my voice, plus I feel very uncomfortable about being recorded while giving readings; you never know what people will do with the recording, especially if they do not like what you have to say.

This story starts while I was doing a Tarot party in a small town in Fife, Scotland.

The lady who had organised the party had brought out an old-fashioned tape machine, you know the ones, those where you have to press play and record at the same time!

Each person had their own cassette to record their readings. I have never been comfortable with this. As each person came and went, it was becoming increasingly difficult to focus on the readings. In my mind I was asking myself 'how are you going to sound on tape?', whilst being mindful not to say something which may be offensive or be misconstrued by someone listening back to the recording.

Eventually the night was coming to an end. I had just one reading remaining. This was the reading for the person who owned the home.

As always Margaret was there, bringing in the family members from the spirit side, getting the names and showing me how they died. I was able to determine from what the spirits were showing me that the lady who was getting the reading had lost a child many years before. Her gran, Bella, was in the room coming forward to say that the baby was safe, and that she was there to take the baby over.

As the reading went on, I noticed in the corner of my eye that there was another spirit in the room. I could sense movement but could hear no words. Even Margaret could not tell me what was being said. My focus was being blurred by the tape machine recording what was being said. During the reading I did pick up that the woman had a 15-year-old daughter who was being a bit of a rebel. I explained that her gran was telling me that she needed to rein her daughter in a bit. I also picked up that her father was ill, but I could sense that he would make a full recovery.

Having given all the information I was able to, I ended the night. Feeling totally shattered, I said my 'goodbyes' and headed home.

It was a couple of weeks later that the lady who owned the house came in to see me. She had booked a readying with me. I explained that I normally ask people to wait at least 6 months between readings. She explained that it was really important that she saw me. Her 15-year-old daughter had died during an attack, and she needed me to connect with her. She was also keen for me to listen to the tape she had brought in.

I was shocked by the sad news. I warned the woman that it may be too soon for her to attempt to contact her daughter, but that I would ask Margaret to see if the girl's grandmother had taken her over.

She sat down in my reading room and took out the tape machine. Placing it on my table, she reminded me that when we started the reading, we had tested the tape by recording 'Testing, testing, 1, 2, 3'. We had played back the test recording to check that all was working. The test recording had worked without a problem.

'Listen to this', she said nervously. She pressed 'play' to play the tape.

There was a silent crackle and then the heavy breathing started. It was like a faint growl, which was barely audible.

Neither the reading nor our conversation at the time could be heard; there was nothing but the sound of growling and heavy breathing. I looked up, amazed.

'Wait for it!', she said. A few seconds later, a chilling voice could be heard. It spoke long drawn-out words. 'Raaaaape. Raaaape. Raaaaape'. This continued through the tape recording until we started to smell rubber burning. Looking down at the cassette player, I could see a small amount of smoke coming from the tape deck. I quickly hit the stop button, but it was too late; the tape had been damaged irreparably.

'Oh my God!', the woman cried. 'I can't believe it!'. 'What happened to your daughter?', I asked. She went on to explain that her daughter had been sneaking out at night at the weekend. She had been going into town to the local night club. On the way back she had been sneaking through the local church yard as a short cut. However, 3 weeks ago, she was attacked and murdered whilst on her way home. She started to sob. I handed her a tissue and asked her whether the police had managed to catch the perpetrator. 'Yes', she replied. 'They have arrested a convicted rapist, who had just been released from prison'.

'I am so sorry to hear', this I said. 'I can ask Margaret to see if she can connect with your daughter'. She nodded desperately.

I summoned Margaret who appeared in front of me with a face that could turn milk sour! I asked her if she could see if the woman's daughter had crossed over.

A few minutes later I started to get a vision of the woman's daughter in 'the in-between'. This is where I believe spirits go when the first die; some call it the valley of death, and so on.

She looked alone and afraid. I tried reaching out to her, but she was scared. I then saw Margaret, who had brought Bella, the girl's grandmother with her. The girl looked over to her Gran who was waiting with her arms stretched out. Bella welcomed her granddaughter with the kind of loving embrace that only a grandmother can offer.

'Thanks Margaret', I said. I opened my eyes and turned to the lady. 'Your daughter has crossed over and is at peace with her gran, Bella', I reassured her.

The lady was overwhelmed with emotion and grief. After a hot cup of tea, she thanked us for our work. She did offer to pay but I refused. Sometimes it's not right to charge. This was one of those occasions.

After a long time pondering the incident, I was convinced that because of being recorded, my focus was being on the recording. As a result of this, I was unable to pick up on any warnings being given by the spirit.

I believe that if you are also recording while working with spirit, the spirit can latch on to the recording. This may result in the spirit, attached to the physical recording, coming home with you.

From that day on, I have not allowed people to record their readings on any form of recording device, physical or digital.

It someone wants a record of what has been said, I let them use a good old-fashioned pen and paper.

With modern technology, there are apps and software which permit "ghost hunters" to catch audio of spirit talking. Whilst the net contains many interesting clips, this remains a practice I will not indulge in.

Honey don't do it, think of the kids

Being brought up as a Jehovah's Witness, you are constantly being told that there are no such things as the spirits of the dead; that it is all the devil and his demons trying to hurt people. Still today my own parents, God love them, will even say the same thing; 'it's the devil causing harm and its the demons that control the readings'.

I disagree 100%. If this was true, then there would be no good news, or hope coming from the spirits, or via any means of divination. This next case is solid proof to me that divination and contact with the spirits can bring love and hope when it is done in a respectful and proper manor.

A few years ago, a gentleman in his early 40s had booked a reading with me. I don't often get men coming for readings, mainly woman. It's always nice to see a man who is open minded enough to have a reading independently.

The guy came in. He looked professional but was extremely nervous. I shuffled the cards and asked him if he could shuffle them too. This was a strange reading situation, as Albert appeared in the corner of the room. This automatically puts me on edge, as this is a sign that something not good or negative is going to happen.

After picking his seven cards, I started to do the reading. Let's call the man Trev. I could see that Trev had lost his mother from cancer many years ago, when he was just a small boy. He had been brought up by his father, who had turned to drinking heavily. His father was quite emotionally and physically abusive towards both Trev and his sister.

I saw that he had 3 children, two boys and a girl (aged 12, 9 and 6). It was at that point that a lady had come into the room. 'Hi, I'm Emma', she said. 'I am his wife. Please tell him I'm ok'.

I looked at the gentleman and explained to him that I had a lady here in spirit who says her name is Emma. 'She tells me she is your wife and that she is ok', I explained. Trev started to sob. 'I miss her so much, and the kids keep crying for her'.

It's extremely hard to remain calm during this type of reading. It is important that I remain in total control of my own emotions. I asked if

Emma had died because of a blood clot to the brain. 'Yes', he replied. 'I'm struggling to cope', he continued.

It was then that Albert walked over. He was holding a rope with a hangman's noose on the end. I could see him placing it around Trev's neck. My vison went blurred for a second or two. When it returned, I saw Trev hanging from a beam in his garage. I looked up and could see the three children in foster care all upset and distressed.

I shook the vision and looked back at Trev who was sitting, crying in front of me. I took his hand and held onto it. I looked him in the eyes. 'I see that you are going to hang yourself in the garage', I said. 'Yes', he replied. 'I have been thinking about it for days. I can't let myself become like my dad. I cannot put my kids through what I had to go through!'.

Emma walked over to him and asked me to remind him of each of their children's births. To remind him about how proud and loving he was to their children. She urged me to tell him that she loved them all with all her heart and that she is with them all each day. She went on to say that she wanted him to take that love and to shower their children with it; to remind them each day that they are so very loved. She said she knew he was strong enough to do so.

After I had relayed what Emma had said, he broke down in tears. He said that's what she had made him promise he would do before she died.

I explained to him that his children needed him more than ever.

He calmed down and asked me to tell Emma that he would go on and be the best father he could be.

Albert at this point turned and left the room. With that silence, the reading ended.

Last year Trev booked in again for a reading. He was a totally different man. He told me that he still misses Emma every day, that he talks to her and keeps her memory alive with their children. He told me that he had just met someone new and was happy. He informed me that his children all liked her too which was an added bonus.

This case proves to me that readings can't be controlled by evil or dark forces. If this was the case, they would have allowed Trev to have committed suicide and to destroy his family. It was the love of his dead wife, and Albert's vision that stopped him from taking that fateful step. Because of this, Trev has now found happiness and he has been able to adjust his life for the greater good.

It still puzzles me that even though Albert maybe a demon, he does not portray himself as such. Maybe there is hope that light does win against the darkness. Albert's conduct continues to concern me. He has been playing up more recently and has been angry and rude. Only the other day while I was doing a reading, for example, Albert was standing in the corner of the room growling and hissing to himself. Halfway through the reading he decided to knock my wedding picture off my desk which in turn freaked out the lady who was getting the reading. After calming her down, I had to explain that Albert was having a bit of a hissy fit, as I was not giving him any attention.

KICKING THE BIN NOT THE BUCKET

This next case has a bit of a comical aspect to it. Even though it is a serious case of possession, I still chuckle when I think about it.

I received a call from one of our clients asking if I could come round and have a look around their house as there were a few strange things going on in the daughter's bedroom. After seeing what my availability was, I agreed to go and see what it was.

On the day of the visit, one of my volunteers turned up to the centre and decided that she wanted to come along as well. My volunteer, (let's call her Di), was very much liked, a bit clumsy, but very lovable. She asked if it would be ok to come along, I agreed as long as she did what I said and didn't get in the way!

When I turned up at the house, I looked up at the bedroom window. I could feel straight away that this was the room where the problems were.

The householder answered our knock with a look of relief. She literally dragged me into the house. 'Oh my God! I'm so relived you came; I have been freaking out'. the young mother cried.

I could tell straight away that there had been serious going on here. Even as I entered the house, I could sense immediately that there was something evil lurking in the house.

Standing in the hallway with Di, the front door slammed shut on its own. 'Bloody hell' cried Di as she pushed passed me, running into the woman's living room.

'That's fine Di. You stay in there where it's safe' I shouted to Di, straightening myself back up after having been flung against the wall.

'It's up here', a voice said. I looked up and there was Margaret. She was standing on the landing, pointing to the room which I had spotted as we approached the house.

'Ok', I called back. 'I will be up in a minute'.

The owner of the house looked at me puzzled. I guess it does look bizarre when you see someone talking to nothing!

I went into the front room and asked the woman what had been going on.

'It started about 4 months ago', the woman started. 'my daughter, who is 5, started crying during the night. She was waking up in her room screaming. This was waking her little sister who has the bunk bed below'.

I asked the mother if her daughter had said what she is hearing or seeing. 'She tells me that there is a bad man in her room. He stands by the window and keeps shouting at her', she replied.

I enquired whether there had been any physical attacks. 'Yes', she replied 'on her back there were pinch marks. They were in places she can't reach herself. I know her little sister hasn't done this'.

I looked up and could see Di having a bit of a panic attack. 'Can you take me home, please?' she asked. 'I'm blooming scared to death being here'.

I was getting slightly annoyed as she had asked to come, knowing what we were going to. 'No', I replied. 'You wanted to come, so you have to see it through'.

I had had a feeling that she would be like this. I must admit, it was a bit funny seeing her freaking out it; naughty I know, but I had warned her.

I looked back over at the woman and asked if anything else had been happening in the house. The lady went on to tell be that there had been several things going on over the last few months. Her husband was suffering with ill-health, having extreme tummy problems and being in constant pain. Things had been going missing in the house; the TV had also turned itself on in the night. I asked if it was around 3am. She confirmed this. She went on to tell me that the other day she had been in the bathroom and when she looked in the mirror, she had seen a shadow behind her. At that point, she had felt a sharp stinging pain on her face. When she looked in the mirror, she had three scratch marks on her face.

She explained that several times she had woken up in the night to the smell of burning. Every time this happened, it was 3am. She said that when she went to the kitchen to check all was ok, she felt that there was something watching her.

I looked up and Di was now green. 'I feel sick' she said. It was as though I was babysitting for her, but not getting paid!

I gave her my car keys and told her to go and wait in the back of my car. This she did unquestioningly.

Margaret shouted down at me 'Are your coming up stairs? We have work to do!'.

'Ok give me a minute', I shouted in response.

I looked at the lady and told her what I felt what was going on. 'I think you have a possession here; an entity or evil spirit has entered your home and is draining your energies and ripping you family apart. I feel that you, your husband and daughters are in danger at the moment'.

I reassured her not to panic as we would perform a house cleansing. I told her that if there was a possessed item, we could remove it.

I took out my sage and crucifix and blessed salt. I opened the windows on the ground floor and went upstairs. I went into the daughter's room. Margaret was standing in the corner. 'You took you time' she chastised. 'It's as plain as the nose on your face! The possessed item is the doll in the window. There is an evil spirit attached to it', she explained.

Yet again, it was one of those horrible porcelain dolls that everyone in the 80s and 90s thought were great.

The house owner was behind me. 'Where did that doll come from?' I asked. She explained that her parents had bought it from a jumble sale 5 months previously. She had put it there for her daughter. Even though the daughter did not like it, her mother still insisted it stayed there.

I looked at the doll and could feel straight away that it was possessed. I asked the lady to go downstairs and fetch a bin bag. I planned to use this to put the doll in; the doll had to be removed from the house.

As I picked the doll up, I felt a burning sensation on my hand. Taking a closer look, I could see small scratch marks on my hand above my thumb. The burning sensation also started on my neck. I could only imagine that the entity was doing this to try to scare me.

'I am not afraid of you', I declared. 'I'm not a little girl who you can scare and hurt. Now back, off or Margaret and me will send you somewhere from which you can't come back from".

The demon in the doll hissed as I put it into the black bin bag. I then took the bag downstairs and put it outside the front door.

As soon as I walked back into the house, I could feel that the heavy darkness was lifted and peace had returned to the house. I took out the sage, lit it and started doing the cleansing starting with the living room and then working my way to the daughter's bedroom.

Sitting down with the house holder, I explained that she would always be vulnerable to spirit attack, that she had to take steps to protect herself and her family. I advised that she should never bring second-hand dolls into her home again.

She was extremely grateful for my help. After explaining that she must keep her home cleansed, I said my goodbyes and left, with the demon doll in the bin back.

Opening the back door of my car, Di looked rather distressed but thankfully she was no longer green.

Placing the bag on the seat next to Di I gave her strict instructions not to open the black back. As I got in the driver's seat and pulled off, Di opened the bag! The next thing I knew she was screaming with all the power of her lungs. Swerving the car and pulling over I looked back.

'What the hell is going on?' I asked.

'I opened the bag. I pulled out the doll and its head turned to look at me. The doll bit my finger!', Di shrieked.

Looking at her hand, I could see that she did indeed have a bite mark on her finger.

The only thing I could think of to deal with this was to salt and burn the doll. Bagging the doll back up I drove to a friend's house. I knew this friend had a garden bin furnace which I would be able to use to destroy the doll.

Pulling up at the house, I grabbed the bag and with Di reluctantly following me, I ran to the back garden. My friend came out and agreed that we could destroy the doll in the furnace. I opened the lid of the furnace and as I lifted the bag to put the doll in, I started to feel light-headed, with pains developing in my chest. Margaret appeared to my right. 'Hurry up and get the little bugger in that bin', she said.

I mustered all my strength and pushed the doll into the bin. I sprinkled some blessed salt and squirted some lighter fuel on top. I lit a match and dropped it in. As the flames rose, I started to recite the Lord's Prayer.

The flames started to rise through the funnel of the furnace. The flames were colours that I had never seen; they were purples, reds and yellows. Even Di was shocked by the colours.

As I was nearing the end of the Lord's Prayer, the doll started to kick the side of the bin. A piercing scream could be heard, coming from inside the furnace. I must admit it was scary. I could hear a voice in my head screaming.

Margaret held out her hands, facing the furnace and started to chant, 'I commit you, evil being, back to the pits of hell, back to where you came from'.

I put my hands up, facing the furnace which was still banging with the kicking noise.

'In the name of all that is good, I send you back to hell', I cried. It was then that the kicking stopped, and the flames died down. I looked at Di, her face frozen in fear.

Through her fear, Di mumbled, 'I can't believe what I have just seen! I'm really shocked and don't think I will ever sleep again!'.

Even though this was a serious case I still chuckle at Di's reaction. I think she learnt a lesson that day; not to open a Pandora's box.

The lesson here is also that we should always be careful about what we bring into our house; always make sure you cleanse a second-hand item with salt or sage first.

If you are still unsure, do not let it into your house. Say 'no' and walk away.

Many house possessions occur because people bring items into their houses that have a spirit attached to them. These are sometimes called conduits. These items when brought into the home act as a portal for spirits or demons.

It is vital that you identify the item as soon as possible.

There are several ways of dealing with these.

Using salt and then burning the item will destroy the item, but the entity or spirit will still survive. You can, however, do an exorcism on the item to release the entity from it, and then salt and burn it.

As an alternative, you can take the item and keep it in a blessed and secure place, where the entity or spirit can cause no harm.

Either way you need to get it out of your house!

SCREAM, YOU'RE ON CANDID CAMERA

Living in a 16th century house with a graveyard in your back garden comes with numerous different problems. My time living in Kirk Wynd has resulted in many creepy stories. This next chapter is a collection of some of the happenings from the short time I lived there.

The house in question was a 3-floor house which was first built for a Dutch merchant around the 16th century. Over the years the property had a multitude of different uses, from an orphanage, an army recruitment centre to nurses' residence.

The history of the house was clouded in strange deaths and a murder. It did not matter which part of the house I was in, I always had that feeling that I was being watched. When people used to visit, they would invariably say that they had the feeling that they were being watched; most would say they felt as if they were being pushed when descending the 3rd floor stairs.

I later found out that a lady had been murdered by her husband. He had pushed her down the stairs and this caused her neck to break. He then killed the children and proceeded to hang himself in the attic. I was unable to validate this 100%, however the comments from multiple visitors added weight to this theory; some would say that they could see children in the corner of their eyes, or that they felt as if a small hand was trying to hold their hand.

My bedroom was on the top floor with the door to attic being in my room. At night I used to sleep with the hall light on, as I was scared to be there. It's daft, I know, but this house made me very uncomfortable as the negative energies were very overwhelming.

At night as I lay in bed, I could see the light shining in from the hallway through the gap at the bottom of the bedroom door. Every now and then I would catch a glimpse of someone walking past the door. They would walk back and forth all night.

One night I decided to go to the door. Placing my ear at the door, I could hear heavy breathing on the other side.

Lying in bed I would often be woken by the sound of banging and footsteps from the attic.

It sounded like small children running up and down.

Just make sure in your own home that if you decide to sleep with a light on that you are prepared to see something you may not want to see in the shadows created.

I recall one occasion when my friend Dawn from Newcastle had come for a visit. She was at the home and doing some work on the computer for me. She was sitting with her back to the door. She recounted sitting with her door to the back. On hearing a voice asking, 'how are you getting on?', she turned around to see who was there. There was, however, no-one to see. She left the room and looked around the rest of the ground floor, where she was working. The whole place was empty apart from her, or so she thought!

It's interesting to note that Margaret never appeared at this house. Even when I tried to summon her, she would not appear. I believe the house was poisonous and evil and this prevented Margaret from materialising. Albert, however, appeared several times; especially when I did readings for others at the house. I would often catch him in the attic; he seemed to like the energy up there.

I think that the scariest experience I had in the house was when I had a visit from my second oldest sister. We had put cameras up in the attic to live stream and record what was going on in that space. One evening Dawn, my sister and I were on the first floor watching the live feed. We sat for several minutes watching the orbs floating around, moving up and down, side to side. It was very interesting to watch their movements. After several minutes, my sister commented that it was getting a bit boring just watching orbs. I agreed. It was at this exact moment, that we all saw the white figure of a man walk past the camera. It appeared to us as clear as day. As the figure passed the camera it turned and looked at us directly through the lens. Chills ran through us. We were so scared that we were hugging onto each other like limpets. I think it's fair to say that we were really shitting ourselves!

The more time I spent living in the house on Kirk Wynd, the more I drained, tired, and fatigued I felt. I was starting to have regular night terrors where I would wake up and there would be a shadow demon hovering above me. It took all of my effort to get rid of it. I felt vulnerable and depressed. I had lost a lot of weight and felt weaker by the day.

I tried to cleanse the house constantly, but it made no difference. In the space of 6 months. I lost three good friends to cancer. Coincidence? I feared not. I had to make the decision to move.

Leaving Kirk Wynd was like having a heavy weight lifted off me. Once in my new home my sleep pattern improved. Margaret was back and was working with me again. Things were back on the up.

SANDRA IN BATH

This is a modern-day story set here in Redditch where I am currently living. It starts when I first moved into my husband's house.

During the first months together, we were having a conversation about the paranormal and what was in and around the house. I explained to my husband that there was a lady in the bath who had been stabbed and had her throat slit; she had been murdered a couple of hundred years ago.

My husband found this hard to believe. The house was only a few years old, and he was the first buyer of the house. 'How on Earth could there be the spirit of a woman in the bath, when I am the first owner of the house?', he asked. I explained that she could have been murdered on the land and for some unknown reason she was appearing in our bath.

One night whilst I was in the bath, I was talking to my husband about Sandra. My husband was on the toilet. When he had finished, he stood and declared, 'hey Sandra, cop a look at this!' before dressing. I warned him that it was not the best idea to make fun of or mocking the dead. I urged caution as Sandra would get him. This went over the top of his head.

It was around a year after this that we were having an event at the clinic. I called these events 'Spooky nights'. These involved scary stories, table tipping, ghost hunting. The evenings finished with a session on the Ouija board.

Although my husband was not willing to take an active part, as a dutiful partner he supported by serving tea and coffee, or by helping in the shop.

During the Ouija sessions my husband would never touch the board. He was happy to write the letters down letter by letter whilst attempting to decode the intended message. During the session this particular evening, we had around eight people using the board. They were all taking it in turns in groups of four. (Please remember Ouijas boards are safe as long as you have someone experienced with you and always respect the board and the spirits). It is important to note that those in attendance were clients and were not personal friends of my husband and me.

During the session on the Ouija board, everyone in attendance received a message from someone they knew who had passed over. Towards the end of the session, I asked if there were any more spirits that had a message and who the message was for.

The board then spelt out my husband's name. There was nobody else with this name in the room. It was at this point that I took my finger off the glass. I asked for one of the other attendees to take over. I did not want my husband to think I was influencing the board.

The girl who took over asked the board what the message was. The board answered, 'Get out of the house'. The girl asked, 'Why does he need to get out of the house?'. The answer from the board was 'because I am going to harm you'. This threat of violence seemed to delight the group! My husband was not as happy!

The girl leading the séance continued by asking 'Why do you want to harm him, he is a lovely person!'. The board then spelt out, 'he mocks me'. Again, there was delight amongst many of the attendees at this response!

'Who is this?' the girl asked. The board replied "Sandra, in the bath'.

It was at this point that I looked over towards my husband. He was clearly visibly distressed by what he had witnessed even to the point of being angry at being there in the first place.

We closed down the board and cleansed the room. The delighted attendees started to pack up and go home, pleased and happy at my husband being terrorised (or maybe sheer relief that it had not been them!).

My husband was so distressed, that he declared he was too scared to go home. I explained that there were consequences to upsetting the spirits as spirits can harm and kill you. I accept this was not being overly helpful in calming my distressed husband. I told him that he could redeem himself by taking some rose quartz to the bathroom and by apologising to Sandra for mocking her.

When we got home, my husband sheepishly went upstairs to the bathroom with the rose quartz. I could hear him apologising to Sandra 'I'm sorry for mocking you, Sandra. I didn't mean it and I won't ever do it again. I'm sorry you died in such a terrible way'. He then came hurtling back down the stairs. It's funny but we are not allowed to mention Sandra again in the house. Now my husband is a believer and he will never mock the dead again. To this day, he reports that he is anxious using the toilet in the bathroom and wonders if Sandra is there watching him.

From this true story, we see that it is really important not to be disrespectful to the spirits of those who have passed over. This is especially important if there have been traumatic circumstances to their death. A traumatic death can sometimes turn spirits twisted and evil and mean that they will willingly cause you harm or distress.

It's a good idea to check what has gone on in your home, or the land around before moving in. If you find evidence of wrong-doing or evil, ensure that the house is cleansed and make peace with any entities.

Conclusion

Going back to the original story at the start of the book, Ann and I managed to pull ourselves together and we banished the spirits in Mrs Renaults home. Ann gave birth to a healthy baby boy. She never accompanied me on a cleansing again after that little tumble down the stairs....

I hope that you have enjoyed the stories in this book. These are just some of the most memorable experiences I have had whilst dealing with spirits.

Today Margaret still helps me with readings, house cleansing and exorcisms. However, the older I get, the more difficult these things become. My energy and strength are not as good as they used to be.

I hope these stories have shown you that spirits of the dead are real, evil is real, and demons do exist. Many people spend so much time believing in good, angels, God and so on, yet they deny the existence of evil, and demons. Whether you choose to believe or not, this book is my testimony that spirits and demons are real. They are all around us, waiting for the opportunity to strike.

Rest assured that the majority of people will never experience what I do in seeing spirit, panic not! Remember, however that you need to play your part to keep it this way. Never provoke or invite evil or negativity into your home.

Be wary of second-hand items.

Be respectful when using tools of divinations, especially Ouija boards. Never drink alcohol or do drugs when using them.

Be aware of waking up at 3am in the morning if you are disturbed or wake up with that heavy feeling. If this happens at 3am seek help and cleansing.

At night, avoid looking at the back seat of your car when looking in the rear-view mirror; especially when driving through creepy areas.

Use your intuition and if something does not feel right avoid it.

It's time now for me to say 'thank you' for taking the time to buy and time to read my book. I hope it has given you something to think about!

Night, night out there whatever you are, and remember turning on the lights at night won't help you…..

Printed in Great Britain
by Amazon